Succeeding

as a

Super Busy

Parent

75 PRACTICAL TIPS FOR BALANCING
LIFE, LOVE, KIDS, AND CAREER

Natalie R. Gahrmann

ISBN 0-7414-1316-7

Published by:

INFINITY
PUBLISHING.COM

1094 New DeHaven Street, Suite 100
West Conshohocken, PA 19428-2713
Info@buybooksontheweb.com
www.buybooksontheweb.com
Toll-free (877) BUY BOOK
Local Phone (610) 941-9999
Fax (610) 941-9959

Printed in the United States of America

Printed on Recycled Paper

Published January 2005

This book is dedicated to my loving and supportive family and to all the parents who work so hard to be the BEST they can be. And, to all children—may you have the path created for your true happiness by having parents who are more joyous, fulfilled, and successful.

ACKNOWLEDGMENTS

- To my *husband and best friend*, Rich. Without his belief in me and his ongoing support, I could not have written this book.

- To my *wonderful children* Matthew and Kaitlyn, whose love inspires me to be the best (parent) I can be.

- To my *parents*, Betty Rosenthal and Jerome Rosen, for helping me learn how to believe in myself and to use my talents and gifts to their fullest.

- To my *in-laws*, the Gahrmann family, for always making me feel like a vital part of their family and for getting excited about the possibilities of this book.

- To *my clients*, for trusting in our relationship and utilizing your strengths and talents to their fullest. For being a model of what is really possible.

- To the *readers* of my *"Practical Tips for Working Parents"* e-newsletter, for their feedback and for keeping me inspired and motivated while I wrote practical and timely tips each week. Also, for the guidance to help determine the best format and content for this book.

- To *BlueSuitMom*, especially Maria Bailey and Rachael Bender, for providing me with the opportunity to be your work/life expert. And, to those who requested my expert advice, thank you for helping me stay aware of the prevalent issues for working mothers and helping me grow with some of your questions.

- To Melanie Berry of *NetWorking Moms*, for providing an avenue to reach working mothers each week, and for your undying support, encouragement, and friendship.

- To Carol Gerrish of *Transforming Work*, for your friendship and coaching. Thank you for hosting me at your fabulous Web site, www.transformingwork.com.

- To the *Coaching Community*, especially members of the Mom/Coach Special Interest Group, for being role models of what's possible. And, to my coaches...thank you!

- To my *friends, extended family, and neighbors* (you know who you are!) for your support, love, and encouragement both personally and professionally.

- To *my editors*, Deb Cooperman and Pat Hadley-Miller, special thanks for bringing this book new life by helping me speak in my authentic voice and ensuring consistency and professionalism in my writing and my message.

- To *everyone* who has believed in me and my dream to truly help others. By helping parents achieve success and happiness, our children and society will flourish and succeed. Our children are our future!

CONTENTS

FOREWORD

Moms are some of the smartest people you will ever meet in life. For this reason, I feel fortunate to have met millions in my lifetime both personally and professionally. I've met them online through my Web site, www.bluesuitmom.com, in person during one of my work and family balance seminars, on the radio while hosting Mom Talk Radio, or while shuffling my own four children between school and activities. What I've come to learn from all the mothers I've helped along the way is that the challenges of balancing children and life are basically the same for us all. They might take on a number of looks depending on our household make-up or career decisions, but all in all they are the same. It all boils down to one universal goal—how do we balance family, work, life, and self?

What I've also learned in my many years as a busy parent myself is that it's tough to find good help. Sure, you can dig through piles of magazine articles or spend hours reading philosophical books on the subject, but who has the time. Hasn't anyone figured out that we are too busy to search and search for answers? Well finally someone has, and you are holding her book in your hands.

Natalie Gahrmann assembles a comprehensive resource for parents that tackles the universal challenges of busy moms and dads with practical advice that is easily integrated into any household. Natalie connects in a unique way with real-life parents by offering real-life solutions. The stuff you can really apply to your family. A true sign that Natalie appreciates the time-starved parent is her inclusion of Top 10 lists. She does the work for you so you don't have to. This book will become a quick reference guide that will keep you coming back for answers.

Succeeding as a Super Busy Parent will be a resource you use for many years to come. It is a book to keep on a convenient shelf so you can refer to it as your children grow. You will find the answers it provides you to be an invaluable tool for managing your ever-changing role as an individual and parent. There's an answer for every challenge a busy parent faces. The only unanswered question is "What will you do with the extra time you find by following this guide?"

Maria T. Bailey
Founder, BlueSuitMom.com
CEO, BSM Media
Host, Mom Talk Radio
Author: **Marketing to Moms: Getting Your Piece of the Trillion Dollar Market** *(Prima, 2002) and* **The Women's Home-Based Business Book of Answers** *(Prima, 2001)*

PREFACE

Like you, I am a *Super Busy Parent*. My day begins around 4:30 a.m. after my husband leaves for work. I get up, brush my teeth and pop in my contact lenses, get dressed, and make my bed before entering my home office where I work for a couple of uninterrupted hours before the kids wake up. Lately, I've been using most of this time to write *Succeeding as a Super Busy Parent*; in the past I've answered e-mail, meditated, exercised, wrote in my journal, cleaned, organized, and worked on the marketing and administrative aspects of my coaching and training business, *N-R-G Coaching Associates* (www.nrgcoaching.com).

Very often, I've thrown in a load of wash, prepared breakfast, made lunches, worked with a client, and did some writing all before 7:15 in the morning! After my kids get on the school bus, I either continue working or head off to the gym for my workout. Once my daughter gets home from half-day kindergarten, we spend some one-on-one time together, have a friend over or run errands. When my son arrives home, the three of us usually enjoy some concentrated family time. I like to be available to help with homework and give my kids undivided attention in the afternoon.

When my husband gets home from work, we usually have dinner together as a family around 6:30. I love this time because it gives us a chance to reconnect. Now that the kids are getting older, we can't always do this because they often have activities in the evening so we have an earlier dinner before shuttling them off to baseball, dance class, Cub Scouts, or cheerleading. I work two to three nights a week and on Sunday I work a few hours to organize and plan my week, and send out my e-newsletter, *Success Tips for Super Busy Parents*. (For a free subscription, send a blank e-mail addressed to superbusyparent-subscribe@yahoogroups.com.)

After my second pregnancy, I left my job in the corporate world. Although my career was progressing, I decided to take advantage of the opportunity to leave with a severance package because I had become disenchanted with the potential for growth and dissatisfied with the contributions I was making at work. As my work life became unfulfilling, my priorities shifted and time with my family became much more important. Although it may seem like a simple decision, leaving my career was one of the hardest choices I've ever made. I had worked very hard to complete my Masters Degree while working full-time, and had progressed up the career ladder. There were financial, as well as emotional and mental well-being issues that I had to take into account.

Prior to working in the corporate world as a human resources manager and training consultant, I worked several years as a high school business teacher and retail manager. In all of my careers (and personal life) people have always turned to me for help and support, so coaching was a natural transition. When I found coaching (or shall I say, it found me!) it was a blending of the skills, competencies, education, and experience I'd gained throughout my life.

My niche as a success coach quickly became working moms, and later expanded to working parents. Although I work with non-parents too, most people who hire me want to integrate their work and personal/family life and achieve more of their business and personal goals; they want more satisfaction and fulfillment in their career and their life. I became an authority on-line at NetWorkingMoms.com and the work-life expert at BlueSuitMom.com.

As my practice, knowledge and experience continued to grow, I amassed a lot of information that I wanted to share with others in order to help them achieve a better quality of life. I realized that I couldn't possibly work one-on-one with everyone, but I *could* support more people by writing a book. Around this time, my e-newsletter readers began encouraging me to do the same thing. Their suggestions and support helped shape this book; like you, they are *Super Busy Parents*!

When days go well and I tap into my experience and training, I feel worthy of being called an "expert," but being an *expert* is not about being perfect; I've become an expert because I was committed to learning everything I could about the lives of *Super Busy Parents*.

Over the years in my coaching practice and workshops, I've supported hundreds of people and helped them manage their complex lives. By fully experiencing my life, observing people, asking questions, and listening to their answers, I've been able to amass a collection of tips that are real, practical, simple, and fun.

The key to handling the daily responsibilities and conflicting roles as a *Super Busy Parent* can be summed up in the acronym *s-u-c-c-e-s-s* in my *Keys to Success for Super Busy Parents*:

S	**SATISFACTION** with your overall life. Being fulfilled at work, home, and in the other roles in your life.
U	**UNINTERRUPTED** time for you. Time for essential self-care and nurturing.
C	**CONTINUOUS** planning and organizing. Know your priorities. Be flexible and adapt to situations. Be confident about handling life's challenges. Re-evaluate what's working and what's not working so you can make the necessary adjustments. Allow yourself to evolve and grow.
C	**COMMUNICATE** your needs and desires. Determine what you need and let people know. Be willing to re-negotiate. Listen fully to others and respond appropriately.
E	**ENJOY** life. Have fun. Create time for relaxation and personal growth. Live by your values and priorities.
S	Build a **SUPPORT NETWORK** that works for you. Have a variety of people and resources available for you. Discover innovative ways to contribute to others, as well.
S	**SIMPLIFY** your life. Let go of unrealistic standards of perfection and focus on progress instead.

Some days will flow easily and others will offer numerous challenges. I invite you to share your challenges with me; let me know if you have overcome a challenge as a *Super Busy Parent* and how you have handled it. I want *your* tips! I'd love to share your stories on my upcoming Web site (www.superbusyparent.com) and in future books. To contact me, send correspondence to **natalie@superbusyparent.com** or call me in my office at **(908) 281-7098**.

INTRODUCTION

What will success look like for you as a *Super Busy Parent*? Will it mean having more time for yourself? More time for high-quality interactions with your kids? More time for romantic rendezvous with your spouse or significant other? More time to hang out with your friends? Better opportunities in your career? Or, perhaps all of the above?

Whether you're working full-time, part-time or not at all, you have a choice about how to live your life. If your life is stressful and unfulfilling, you can begin re-creating it so that you have more balance, joy, and fulfillment.

This book is designed to be a resource for you—a tool to keep handy. You won't need to read it cover-to-cover (fact is, you probably don't have time for that!). You can skip around and choose tips based on where you feel you can use inspiration and guidance. Realize that there are some tips you may never use and others that will undoubtedly become your favorites. Remember that you can always go backward, forward, or wherever you like in this book so that it supports you when you need it most. You're free to tweak tips and add your own so that you have a comprehensive guide that works exclusively for your needs. Several blank *NOTES* pages have been furnished near the back of this book to provide you with a place to keep your notes, thoughts, feelings, and modified tips.

While everyone is unique, our challenges are often quite similar: How do you get involved in your child's school when you work an hour's drive away? How do you keep your marriage strong when it's been six months or six years since you've had a romantic dinner with your spouse? The overall relationships you have with yourself, your family, friends, and co-workers all help determine how successful you are as a *Super Busy Parent.*

Balance is about living in a way that truly reflects your personal values. It is an evolving process that presents many opportunities to re-evaluate and grow as a human being. Balance is also about autonomy (being self-governing and independent) and the ability to follow through on your promises to yourself and to others. Life is about progress—not about perfection. If you are feeling inadequate, this book will help you acknowledge where you are succeeding in your life. When you do strike a balance that works for you, appreciate the accomplishment of what you've created.

As a success coach in private practice, I've had the opportunity to work one-on-one and in groups with parents who often feel overwhelmed by all the hats they have to wear (for example, being a professional at work, a taxi driver to baseball games and dance classes, a teacher helping their kids with homework, a housekeeper, a cook, a bookkeeper, a shopper, and, oh yeah, a lover to their spouse or significant other). Often at wits' end, they seek out someone like me, a professional trained to motivate people into taking action that will simplify their life, advance their personal or professional goals, and ultimately give their life more meaning—even while lowering their level of stress. I teach people how to optimize their situation so that they can function at their fullest potential in all facets of their life.

The tips in the pages ahead are designed to serve as your *success coach*, as each tip ends with a related action you can take. Some actions are exercises; some involve a conscious thought process, and others offer ways to transform your self-defeating behaviors into more effective ones. Remember, you can try these tips as they are, modify them to fit your current situation, and skip the ones that don't pertain to you. However, in order to produce results, you must take action; nothing will change unless you take conscious and deliberate steps to improve your personal situation.

This book is organized into three sections that focus on helping you transform you, your family, and your work. Self-care and self-knowledge is first because without taking care of yourself you won't have the energy and wherewithal to take care of others or your career.

Your *self* is always there whether you're at work, with family, or alone; devoting time and energy to nurturing your self is highly critical, so don't let your own needs fall through the cracks! This book will help you build a strong personal foundation so that you can tend to yourself and others without guilt or resentment. When you feel good about yourself, your kids are a lot happier with their lives.

A few of my favorite *Top Ten Lists* have been added in *Appendix 1* so that you have a concise summary of tips you can apply in your own life. This will help you quickly find useful practical information when you're in a hurry.

There are a variety of *Recommended Resources* listed throughout this book to help you in obtaining additional support and guidance where you want it. Several Web sites are listed in *Appendix 2*, as well. I've done extensive research to gather the information and compile the suggestions; to my knowledge, they are all accurate at the time of this writing. However, Web sites come and go—if you can't find something I've referred to, use your browser to search for other possible sites. Please notify me of additions or corrections so that I can update my recommendations in later editions of this book. Fortunately for *Super Busy Parents*, many of the suggested books are also available on audiotape, compact disc or in e-book format for easy downloading.

This book will help you strive to be your best. I invite you to use it to help you consciously make choices that benefit you, your family, and your work.

Part 1

BALANCE YOUR PERSONAL LIFE

Life

Quality questions create a quality life. Successful people ask better questions, and as a result, they get better answers.

~ Anthony Robbins

TIP # 1 - EVALUATE YOUR LIFE

We all have the infinite power to shape our destinies. By stepping back from your everyday life and taking stock of what's really important to you individually, in your marriage, and in your family, you can make conscious decisions about how you wish to live your life.

To begin this process, start with your definition of success. *How do you define success?*

Is it measured by:

- the amount of money you earn?
- your job title?
- the size of your house?
- the car you drive?
- the amount of toys you have?
- the amount of time you spend with your family?
- the flexibility you enjoy?
- or, with some other measurement, or a combination of a few? (Be really honest with yourself!)

Some of these things really have nothing to do with who you *actually* are. These things are outside of you and are *external drivers*. The external drivers are often measures of success because they are so easily quantifiable. However, when a good friend or a work colleague is more financially successful, ask yourself what price they might pay for that financial success? Are you willing to pay that price in order to achieve financial success?

Now, consider your life as a whole...

- What is truly important to you?
- What are your dreams?
- How do you spend the majority of your time?
- Where has your life felt out of balance?
- What do you want more of in your life?
- What do you want less of in your life?
- How much achievement, financial wealth, and material things are enough for you?
- When you look back at your life at the end of it, what will make you feel that you've been successful throughout your life?

Related Activity: Begin using a journal to record your thoughts. Writing consistently in a journal will give you a deeper connection with your inner self. Writing will help you have an internal dialogue that clarifies your true feelings. It can also help you alleviate unwanted stress because as you write, you release your innermost thoughts and anxieties and get them out of your head.

When you write in your journal, it's important to ignore your inner critic and avoid censoring your thoughts; write whatever you're thinking and feeling. Begin by writing short passages whenever you can spare a quiet moment. Keep your journal private so that you can communicate without fear of someone else reading it.

To begin journal writing, find a comfortable position, clear your mind, and relax. Then, let your thoughts and emotions flow freely. For this *related activity*, use the questions above to guide your writing and help you determine your individual priorities. Define what you really want for yourself from work, parenting, and from your spouse/partner (if you have one). Then, continue using your journal on a regular basis to help you clarify what you want and stay on track in getting it. Additionally, you can work with a professional coach to get support in getting clear on these issues.

Once you have completed this activity, have your partner perform the same exercise and merge together a shared vision. (Note, this may be difficult and uncomfortable because you are coming to terms with your individual definitions of success, roles, and goals.) You may need to rationalize your individual priorities and agree on how you want to allocate your time.

Recommended Resources

1. *Coach Yourself To Success: 101 Tips For Reaching Your Goals At Work And In Life* by Talane Miedaner (McGraw Hill, 2000)
2. *How A Man Measures Success* by Jim Smoke (Bethany House Publishers, 1997)
3. *The Artist's Way: A Spiritual Path To Higher Creativity* by Julia Cameron (J.P. Tarcher, 2002)
4. *The Handbook Of Journaling: Tools For The Healing Of Mind, Body & Spirit* by Neil F. Neimark, MD (R.E.P. Technologies, 2000)
5. *The Portable Coach: 28 Surefire Strategies For Business And Personal Success* by Thomas J. Leonard (Scribner, 1998)
6. *Write Away: A Journal Writing Tool Kit* by Eldonna Bouton (Whole Heart Publications, 2000)

> *We were made for calm, not chaos, and that is why we long for simpler times. Somewhere deep inside we know that simpler times are better times.*
>
> ~ *Thomas Kinkade*

TIP # 2 - SIMPLIFY LIFE

The life of working parents is often overcomplicated and highly stressed. Through technology you can be "wired" 24 hours a day, seven days per week. Although there are many obvious benefits to technology, there's also a "downside." With cell phones, pagers, and e-mail you can be reached by friends, family, clients, vendors, colleagues, your boss, and your kids. The technology designed to free you ends up controlling you.

Stop validating your sense of worth by filling your life with "stuff." Being busy does not mean that you are any more special or important than anyone else—it simply means that you are busy and probably missing out on the things that would really make you have more joy and fulfillment in your life—the things that are really special and important to you. When your life is overcomplicated and overfull, there is little space for what truly matters. And there's no room for personal growth, positive energy, love, or even breathing at times!

Create more simplicity in your life. Choose to take steps that will move you in the direction of uncomplicating your life. Start by deciding what really matters to you (See Tips #1 & 20) and spend your time and energy doing those things, not just the things that are busywork or that other people expect of you. Ask yourself:

- In what ways is my life chaotic?
- Why is my life so busy?
- What is the hidden payoff for having such a chaotic life?
- What am I building with my current lifestyle choices?
- Is there any future to this lifestyle, or is it actually costing me the kind of future I really want?
- What am I missing out on because I'm choosing to live my life this way?

6

Related Activity: List three big projects, tasks, or commitments and determine a date by which you will eliminate them from your life and free up your energy. Perhaps the clutter in your garage has been bugging you for months, you have an unfinished report to write, you have volunteered to lead a fundraiser for your child's school, or you are on just about every task force or project team at work. Decide what steps you need to take to actually complete the activity. Identify any fears and resistance you have about eliminating the tasks or commitments and work through them. For instance, you may be afraid of getting rid of things that are accumulating in your garage because you might need them someday or they have some type of sentimental value. You may fear retributions at work if you say "no" to participate in a project. Or, you feel a need to keep yourself busy so that you don't have to face something else you're avoiding.

Once you've eliminated some things from your life, do not be tempted to immediately fill that space up with other tasks or commitments. Continue to evaluate all your commitments and responsibilities and focus on the ones that matter.

Recommended Resources

1. *Focal Point: A Proven System To Simplify Your Life, Double Your Productivity, And Achieve All Your Goals* by Brian Tracy (Amacon, 2001)
2. *Simplify Your Life: 100 Ways To Slow Down And Enjoy The Things That Really Matter* by Elaine St. James (Hyperion, 1994)
3. *Simplify Your Life: 101 Ways To Create The Life You'll Love* by Linda Manassee Buell (Simplify Life, 1998)
4. *The 50 Best Ways To Simplify Your Life: Proven Techniques For Achieving Lasting Balance* by Patrick Fanning and Heather Garnos Mitchener (New Harbinger Publishing, 2001)

> *If money is your hope for independence you will never have it. The only real security that a man can have in this world is a reserve of knowledge, experience, and ability.*
>
> *~ Henry Ford*

TIP # 3 - CREATE INDEPENDENCE

By definition, independence is about self-sufficiency, about being autonomous, self-governing, and self-reliant. Independence is about a feeling of freedom. Freedom is formed by attitudes, beliefs, or behavior patterns. The underlying construct for freedom is *time*.

We all have 24 hours in every day. Some of us use this time constructively and productively; others see it slip though their fingers and end up feeling frustrated at having wasted time.

As a working parent, you have many things and people vying for your time and attention. By putting first things first you can allocate your time based on what's most important to you. According to the Pareto Principle (originally developed in the late 1800s by economist and sociologist Vilfredo Pareto), a small number of causes are responsible for a large percentage of the effect, in a ratio of about 20:80.

The theory, known today as the *80:20 Rule*, has stood the test of time and scrutiny, and proven its validity in a number of other areas, too. For instance, in the business world, 20% of a person's effort generates 80% of that person's results. The corollary to this is that 20% of your results absorb 80% of your resources.

In your life, you can dramatically improve productivity by applying this 80:20 rule, too. While the rule is not an absolute, you can use it as a guide and reference point to ask whether or not you are truly focusing on the 20% (the vital few), or the 80% (the trivial many). True progress results from a consistent focus on the 20% most critical objectives. Let go of the other activities that really are not serving you any longer. You'll get more of what you want with less time, money, and energy.

Paul and Sarah Edwards, authors of several self-employment books and experts on working at home, suggest three keys to 80:20 your life:

- Start working with purpose. Define what you are seeking to accomplish.
- Clear out the backlog of things that don't relate or contribute to your purpose.
- Schedule for results based on your goals. Stay focused by keeping your goals visible.

(from Secrets of Successful Self-Employment: Moving From Paycheck Thinking To Profit Thinking, Paul & Sarah Edwards, Simon & Schuster, 1996)

Related Activity: Examine your life and identify the 20% of activities and commitments that provide 80% of your satisfaction and results. Eliminate the 80% that are not satisfying you. By doing so, you'll create more of what you want in your life (e.g., six extra hours in a day, three extra filing drawers, 25% increase in income, and a gigabyte of additional memory on your computer). Carve out 20 minutes each day to celebrate your independence. Consciously choose to take this time to enjoy it, relax, have fun, and refresh your soul and spirit.

Recommended Resource

Secrets of Successful Self-Employment: Moving From Paycheck Thinking To Profit Thinking by Paul and Sarah Edwards (audiotape by Simon & Schuster, 1996)

> *Again and again, the impossible problem is solved when we see that the problem is only a tough decision waiting to be made.*
>
> *~ Robert Schuller*

TIP # 4 - ELIMINATE THE OBSTACLES

We all have hopes, dreams, or goals. Somehow, we never seem to achieve some of them. Obstacles that prevent us from achieving our goals may come from our work life, family obligations, relationships, beliefs, limited resources...virtually anywhere! Unfortunately, as problems arise, we often focus on the problem and don't think about the solution. The more we think about problems, the bigger they seem. By focusing on the problem, we actually decrease our ability to effectively solve it.

It is important to realize that the pathway to a goal is often not straight and direct. There are bumps, potholes, and curves in the road. Your response to the first obstacle often will determine your future on the path and your ultimate success (or failure) at reaching the goal. If you spend too much time focusing only on the problem you may sabotage your chances of ever making it to your goal.

A problem or obstacle may be an opportunity to help you clarify your goal. If you spend your energy focusing on what you want versus what you don't want, you will immediately shift the focus from the problem to the solution. Then, you can think creatively to develop solutions to step around, over, or through the problem that is standing in the way of your goal. Engage both your conscious and subconscious mind to help you find the right answers. Then, you must move into action before your fears grab hold of you and push you back. With effective conscious decisions and actions, you'll undoubtedly achieve your goal.

Related Activity: Determine what obstacles are preventing you from achieving your goals. Look beyond the problem and focus on what you truly want. Then, take new actions toward your goal. Once you've experienced some success in eliminating your obstacles, assist someone else who is stuck on the pathway to their goals by helping them eliminate their obstacles, too.

Recommended Resources

1. *Chicken Soup For The Unsinkable Soul: 101 Inspirational Stories Of Overcoming Life's Challenges* by Jack L. Canfield (Health Communications Inc., 1999)
2. *Getting Through The Day: A Practical Guide To Tapping Internal Resources To Overcome Life's Obstacles Through Imaging And Guided Meditation* by Nancy J. Napier (audiotape by Nancy J. Napier, 1996)
3. *Manifest Your Destiny: The Nine Spiritual Principles For Getting Everything You Want* by Wayne W. Dyer (William Morrow & Company 1999)
4. *Self-Care Now! 30 Ways to Overcome Obstacles That Prevent You From Taking Care of Yourself* by Pauline Salvucci (Pauline Salvucci, 2001)

Overcome the Hurdles!

> *A passionate interest in what you do is the secret to enjoying life, perhaps the secret of a long life.*
>
> ~ *Julia Child (at age 88)*

TIP # 5 - CELEBRATE LIFE

This tip is about rejoicing and celebrating the miracle of life—your life and the lives of your children and those important to you. It's about focusing not on what you do (e.g., being a lawyer, accountant, teacher, or business owner) but on *who* you are. What is it about you that helps others? What do people rely on you for? What do people always seem to turn to you for? How have people utilized your abilities? What functions do you serve in your various roles? For instance, are you a motivator, a listener, a peacemaker, a healer, a problem-solver or a creative thinker? Examining who you "are" rather than what you "do" helps you connect with your main purpose in life.

Rededicate your life to what's truly important to you and align your activities and commitments with your life purpose. You will undoubtedly find more contentment and fulfillment and less stress.

Related Activity: Ignite your passion and purpose in life by connecting with it and using it as a force to inspire your dreams. Live your life with purposefulness! Create hope, excitement, and possibilities in your life.

Define your *life purpose*. Your purpose is about "who" you are—it orients, defines, and identifies you uniquely. It connects to what you see for your future—your vision. Your goals and action steps are a way of keeping your vision clear and available. Be sure your life purpose relates to your vision; *vision* is your view of what you see (your eyes) for the world, your purpose relates to (your heart) who you are and what's important to you.

Next, define your *mission* in life. Your mission is about *how* you will live your vision through your daily actions. It's what you *do* that connects to who you are. It describes how you will achieve the results or outcomes you envision.

Recommended Resources

1. *Living Your Best Life* by Laura Berman Fortgang (Jeremy P. Tarcher/Putnam, 2001)
2. *The Seven Spiritual Laws of Success: A Practical Guide To The Fulfillment of Your Dreams* by Deepak Chopra (Amber-Allen, 1995)

Success for Super Busy Parents

Key Essential #1

SATISFACTION WITH YOUR OVERALL LIFE

Eliminate the obstacles that prevent you from living a fulfilling life. Create more joy, fulfillment, and balance in your life.

Create the Life You Truly Want!

Personal Wellness/Health

> *When a man begins to understand himself, he begins to live. When he begins to live, he begins to understand his fellow men.*
> *~ Noruin G. McGranahan*

TIP # 6 - LOVE YOU FIRST

The most important relationship you will ever have is the one with *yourself.*

The fact is, before you can have great relationships with others, you have to create a great relationship with yourself. We often get so busy and mired down with things to do that we don't get to know ourselves. Getting to know all of you will help you be more accepting of others.

It takes time, patience, persistence, and a willingness to explore not only the bright sunny side, but the dark and not-so-nice sides of yourself. Accept those things about yourself that you've been hard on yourself about; those things that you continually beat yourself up for. Give yourself a break and stop expecting perfection. Every one of us has flaws—as you learn to recognize and accept yours, you will be better able to accept the imperfections in others, as well. Once you get to know yourself fully and create a loving relationship with YOU, it is easier to create those loving relationships with others.

Related Activity: Allow some daily quiet time to discover who you are and what your true gifts are. Tap into your higher wisdom by discovering the wonders and beauty of your inner self. It may take a lifetime for you to get to know yourself fully, but it will be worth it. There are a number of ways you can spend your quiet time each day such as meditating, going for a walk, listening to music, or reading.

One of the most effective ways to get to the inner core of who you are is to write a daily journal (see Tip #1).

Recommended Resource

No Enemies Within: A Creative Process For Discovering What's Right About What's Wrong by Dawna Markova (Conari Press, 1994)

Guard well your spare moments. They are like uncut diamonds.
~ Ralph Waldo Emerson

TIP # 7 - PRACTICE ESSENTIAL SELF-CARE

Your health, attitude, and energy levels are very important to you and to the people around you. It's important to put your needs first in order to take extremely good care of yourself.

What is *essential* for working parents?

Essential self-care entails activities that are designed to totally nurture YOU. These activities can be part of a daily or weekly routine, or they can happen when the need arises. These activities include nourishing your body, mind, and spirit. Essential self-care also includes being sure you get adequate sleep and exercise, eating healthy, and drinking plenty of water. Increasing your level of self-care ultimately allows you to be more generous and supportive of others than you have ever been before because you are honoring your own needs.

Related Activity: Create a list of at least 25 things you would like to do to care for yourself. Make your list comprehensive with actions that can be done daily (like meditation), weekly (like watching a movie), and occasionally (like visiting a friend). After you have made your list, mark next to each item a "B" for body, "M" for mind, "S" for spirit, and "F" for feelings to indicate what aspect of yourself you are caring for when doing the activity. If an item nurtures more than one aspect, designate all that apply. If you realize that there is an aspect not cared for at all, then revise your list to include activities that nurture that area. When you are finished with this list, select five daily, four weekly, and two occasional activities and do them for a month. Be attentive and mindful of the activities you are engaging in and ensure that you are achieving energy and aliveness from those you partake in.

Recommended Resources

1. *Mayo Clinic Guide To Self-Care: Answers For Everyday Health Problems* by Philip T. Hagen, MD (Kensington Publishing Corp., 1999)
2. *Self-Care Cards* by Cheryl Richardson (Cards Edition by Hay House, 2001)
3. *Self-Nurture: Learning To Care For Yourself As Effectively As You Care For Everyone Else* by Alice D. Domar and Henry Dreher (Viking Press, 1999)

Execute Exceptional Self-Care!

Live with intention. Walk to the edge. Listen hard. Practice wellness. Play with abandon. Laugh. Choose with no regret. Continue to learn. Appreciate your friends. Do what you love. Live as if this is all there is.

~ Maryanne Radmacher-Hershey

TIP # 8 - TAKE YOURSELF TO THE DOCTOR

Your physical and mental wellness are not only important to you, but to your family and your work. Schedule an appointment to get a full exam as often as is recommended for your age and known health conditions. When you are experiencing symptoms, don't ignore them hoping they'll go away or because you're worried about the news you may hear. Instead, take the symptoms as your body's way of communicating that there's a problem that needs your immediate attention. Don't ignore the message!

When you choose to ignore the symptoms rather than handling them, they may worsen until the point that you are handling them in a disaster/crisis mode. You'll be putting unnecessary and extra levels of stress on yourself, your work, and the people who love you. You may also cause the situation to worsen beyond repair or treatment.

Everyone will have more time to plan and adjust their lives accordingly when you proactively schedule regular check-ups and have your symptoms checked immediately. Just think of how upsetting it would be for everyone involved if you were suddenly hospitalized, incapacitated, or worse, dead, due to avoiding the message. Many illnesses, diseases, and other conditions are treatable when diagnosed early. Take care of your physical and mental wellness now!

Related Activity: Call today to schedule an appointment with your general practitioner, OB/GYN, internist, dentist, or whoever is appropriate for your personal wellness and medical screenings.

Recommended Resources

1. *Healthwise Handbook: A Self Care Guide For You* by Donald W. Kemper and the Healthwise Staff (Healthwise, 2001)
2. *Self Nurture: Learning To Care For Yourself As Effectively As You Care For Everyone Else* by Alice Domar, PhD and Henry Dreher (Penguin USA, 2001)
3. *Take Care of Yourself: The Complete Illustrated Guide To Medical Self-Care* by Donald M. Vickery and James F. Fries (Perseus Publishing, 2000)

Success for Super Busy Parents

Key Essential #2

UNINTERRUPTED TIME FOR YOU

Learn to nurture yourself without feeling guilty. Find ways to maintain inner harmony, peace, and joy while becoming tremendously successful. Taking time for you is essential to your self-care and allows you to rejuvenate and refresh yourself.

> *As every thread of gold is valuable, so is every moment of time.*
> ~ *John Mason*

TIP # 9 - REDUCE STRESS IN YOUR FREE TIME

With your free time very limited, optimize the time you *do* have by getting more out of it. Try removing your watch at the end of your workday to eliminate the feeling of being ruled by the clock in your spare time. If you've had a particularly hard day, put off discussing important issues with your spouse until later that evening when you're less tense and more open to conversation. Instead, spend quiet time with your family, turn on music, play some games, or just enjoy some time alone. Avoid the television for at least an hour or so to eliminate a bombardment of information and talking.

To feel more in control of your limited free time, complete at least one small task (like de-cluttering a corner of your garage rather than the entire garage) each weekend. Keep the piles and clutter around your house to a bare minimum. When you clear the areas where things pile up you'll clear away tension, as well.

Related Activity: Enjoy your free time to the maximum! Create stress-free opportunities where you focus on having fun. Look at the stresses you've experienced in your life and recall how you've handled them in the past. Indicate ways you can handle your current stresses more effectively and practice, practice, practice!

Recommended Resource

The Simple Living Guide: A Sourcebook For Less Stressful, More Joyful Living by Janet Luhrs (Broadway Books, 1997)

> *You will never find time for anything. If you want time you must make it.*
>
> ~ *Charles Buxton*

TIP # 10 - CREATE YOUR OWN "DOWN-TIME"

Creating your down-time is crucial to you, your family, and your work. It gives you a chance to get re-energized, renewed, and rested. Don't feel guilty about having your own down-time. When your family sees you respecting your own needs by having a time out, they will begin respecting this time, as well.

Here are some ways you can make more time for you:

- Tell your family when and for how long you will be gone.
- Don't let yourself get talked out of *your* time. Unless it's an actual emergency—don't change your plans. Remember that once you're there, you'll be grateful you went.
- Don't feel guilty about taking time for yourself. It is essential! (see Tip #7)
- If you choose not to use your special time, don't blame your family.
- Create space within your home that is for you to enjoy private time, free of interruptions.
- Use music to create a peaceful atmosphere or to drown out other noises while you exercise or meditate at home.
- Delegate more chores around the house to ease your burden of responsibilities.
- Hook up with a friend or two to share your special time (but if they cancel, go anyway!)

Related Activity: Create the down-time that supports and nurtures you.

Recommended Resource

Mommy—CEO (Constantly Evaluating Others): 5 Golden Rules by Jodie Lynn (Martin-Ola Press, 2001)

Physical Environment

TIP # 11 - AVOID BREAKDOWNS

We all have a number of things including our cars, appliances, equipment, tools, and our own bodies that must be maintained regularly to stay in tip-top shape. Maintaining your things by performing regular routine maintenance and upkeep is extremely important for minimizing or alleviating total breakdowns. When something (or someone) is totally incapacitated, it is much more difficult to deal with.

For example, when maintaining your car, you can avoid breakdowns by using your senses to be keenly aware of unusual sounds, poor or sluggish performance, or unusual odors. Within the physical systems, check the fluid levels, filters, batteries, belts, or whatever mechanisms keep it running properly.

If you've ever experienced warning signs right before your kids get really sick, you know exactly what I mean. You'll notice that they become cranky, lethargic, have a slight cough, a sniffle, a body ache, or low-grade fever. I've found that if I become vigilant at these times and insist on extra Vitamin C, rest, a bland diet, and herbal supplements (Echinacea is my personal favorite!) the symptoms never become full blown. In fact, many times the symptoms subside very quickly!

Related Activity: Plan routine care and maintenance appointments at regular intervals for everything and everyone around you that you have control over. Get out your calendar and pencil in tentative dates to target, make appointments, and follow through with the recommended upkeep suggestions from the professionals.

> *Cleaning anything involves making something else dirty, but anything can get dirty without something else getting clean.*
>
> ~ *Dr. Laurence J. Peter*

TIP # 12 - RE-EXAMINE YOUR STANDARDS FOR HOUSEKEEPING

Many of us haven't given up the notion of perfection and high standards for keeping our house clean despite the added pressures and stress caused by the unreasonable expectations of others and ourselves. Your time is far too precious to spend it doing things that really aren't necessary! If you don't have hired help (e.g., a housekeeper, nanny, personal shopper, chef) responsible for the household tasks, it's time to examine how you are spending your time and energy tending to your home. If you're fortunate to have hired help to assist you, make sure they are serving *your* needs.

Begin by looking at the amount of laundry you and your family generate on a regular basis. Having a washer and dryer in just about every home has reduced the scrub and rinse time, but increased the total time spent doing laundry including sorting, carrying, bleaching/spraying, pre-treating, loading, unloading, folding, putting away. The amount of laundry can drastically be cut down by using the same towel for a couple of times after bathing, wearing the same jeans more than once, changing the sheets every two weeks instead of every week, or even running in the same pair of jogging shorts for two days. Be aware of the total time spent taking care of the laundry; far more time is spent than simply the moments of dropping in a load and pushing the button. Also, limit the amount of times you and your family change their clothes on a daily basis. If you haven't already done so, teach every family member (capable of operating the washer and dryer) how to do the laundry.

You can also look at the amount of time and energy you spend completing the tasks to clean your house. There is an old saying that states that tasks expand according to the time allotted to them; if you have five hours it takes five hours, when you have only an hour you can accomplish the major stuff in just the hour!

There are four basic principles to keep in mind when it comes to home maintenance, according to Dianna Booher, author of *Get a Life Without Sacrificing Your Career* (September 1, 1996, McGraw Hill):

- Clean only WHAT you need to clean.
- Clean only WHEN you need to clean it.
- Have ALL THE TOOLS YOU NEED (cleaners, rags, brushes and mops) in one carrier.
- For the huge cleaning projects (like windows, the garage, vacuuming the upholstery and drapes) that need to be done only a few times a year, consider HIRING SOMEONE by the hour.

(Reproduced with permission of the McGraw-Hill Companies)

Related Activity: Take a new perspective about how clean your house and clothes really need to be. If you're entertaining guests or having prospective buyers come through with their realtor, your standards may undoubtedly be higher than the norm. Look around your house and diagnose the amount of true dirt and clutter that exists. Follow simple spot cleaning principles by cleaning only what requires your attention. Start keeping your house extremely well-organized with things in their proper place so that you can actually go a lot longer between cleanings.

Recommended Resources

1. *Making A Home: Housekeeping For Real Life* by Better Homes and Gardens Editors (Meredith Books, 2001)
2. *Get A Life Without Sacrificing Your Career: How To Make More Time For What's Really Important* by Dianna Booher (McGraw Hill, 1996)

> *The Three Rules of Work: (1) Out of clutter find simplicity (2) From discord find harmony (3) In the middle of difficulty lies opportunity.*
> ~ *Albert Einstein*

TIP # 13 - ELIMINATE CLUTTER

Look at the spaces in your work and your home life and everything in between, including your car and your briefcase to determine areas you can de-clutter. With life being so busy, piles accumulate, files seem to multiply, toys are overflowing from the toy box, and clothes are bursting from drawers and closets.

One of the easiest and most effective ways to attract something that you desire into your life is to create the space. Clutter may not appear as much of an inhibitor to your success, but clutter keeps you in a state of confusion. Whatever you need to do to get rid of clutter in your life, make a commitment and do it! It will make a huge difference in the way you think and feel. Removing clutter allows for more space in your life, both in time and freedom.

Conquering clutter is an ongoing battle for most busy people. Here are a few ideas to get you started:

- Go through your (electronic and paper) files and discard old memos, reports, and articles that you've been saving "just in case."
- Make it a habit (for you and everyone else) to always put things back where they belong.
- Do not bring junk mail into your home or office; get removed from as many mailing lists as possible. (Note: you can contact the American Direct Marketing Association, www.dmaconsumers.org/offmailinglist.html, to have them remove you from their lists for a nominal fee; you can contact the sender directly; and indicate that you don't want to be included on their mailing lists; or, you can indicate your preference for exclusion from future mailings when ordering a product/service, or filling out a warranty card, or making a donation)

- Clip out and file the articles from magazines that interest you and recycle or discard the rest of the magazine.
- Give away or sell unwanted toys and other items you (or your kids) are no longer interest in. (You know what they say about one person's trash being someone else's treasure!)
- Load up a bag of clothes that don't fit, are out of style, or are just plain unflattering and take them to a local charity, shelter, or rummage sale.
- Get rid of the little things, like clothes, furniture, and books, and it will be easier to get rid of the bigger things, such as an unfulfilling job or a relationship that really isn't right for you.

You pay a high price for living with clutter in your life because it makes it hard for you to function at 100%; it keeps you stuck and keeps you busy looking for things rather than getting things done. Creating space contributes to feeling better physically, mentally, and emotionally.

Related Activity: Conquer clutter by spending a half-hour to an hour each day for a week (or weekend) just clearing out stuff you no longer want or need. If possible, enlist the help and support of your family and work colleagues in this goal. Start small with one shelf or one closet and enjoy the feeling of accomplishment as you begin creating space in your life. Gain momentum and keep it going by preventing yourself from getting overwhelmed or quitting before you experience the results. Then, move on to the next area until you've gone through every room and space in your home and at work. By eliminating things you no longer need, you will spend remarkably less time looking for things and you will have the opportunity to reach your full potential.

One of my favorite techniques for clearing physical clutter is to start with three boxes labeled: *throw away, give away,* and *keep.* Quickly go through a filing cabinet, closet, or drawer and place items in the appropriate boxes. If you're really uncertain and afraid of discarding—create another box labeled with the contents and date. If items are not used within a year from the date indicated, reconsider discarding at that time. It's essential to shift your attitude to "it's okay to throw away" in order to conquer clutter.

Recommended Resources

1. *Clutter Control* by Susan Wright (Barnes & Noble Books, 1999)
2. *Let Go Of Clutter* by Harriet Schechter (McGraw Hill Professional, 2000)
3. *Stop Clutter from Stealing Your Life: Discover Why You Clutter And How You Can Stop* by Mike Nelson (New Page Books, 2000)

Success for Super Busy Parents

Key Essential #3

CONTINUOUS PLANNING & ORGANIZING

Strive for progress rather than perfection. Allow yourself to evolve as you continuously evaluate what's working (& not). Make the necessary adjustments to improve your situation.

> *A first-rate organizer is never in a hurry. He is never late. He always keeps up his sleeve a margin for the unexpected.*
>
> *~ Enoch Arnold Bennett*

TIP # 14 - ORGANIZE AT HOME AND WORK

How your physical environment functions is more important than how it looks. If you feel happy and comfortable in your space, and can find what you need immediately without wasting precious time and energy looking for it, then you are well-organized. For years the benchmark for an organized home or office was more about cleanliness than about the environment itself. True organization enables you to live, work, and relax exactly as you want to. When you are organized, your home, office, and schedule all reflect and encourage who you are, what you want, and where you are going.

Effective organizing begins with the big picture. It reflects how you think, how you relate to the world, how you pace yourself, how you like to operate, and your sense of visuals. Don't wait until you've reached the breaking point and can no longer stand your children's closets or toy chests, or, your filing cabinets, closets, drawers and piles of mail. Don't look for instant relief when you can no longer stand the mess. Instead, start today by developing a plan that reflects who you are, how you like to operate, and your specific situation and needs. Your organizing system will work effectively when you spend time analyzing the situation(s) and planning your personal course of action.

Related Activity: To help you organize your life, develop and implement a plan that reflects who you are, how you like to operate, and your specific situation and needs.

Recommended Resources

1. *Order From Chaos: A Six-Step Plan For Organizing Yourself, Your Office, And Your Life* by Liz Davenport (Three Rivers Press, 2001)

2. Check the *Professional Organizers Association* for local resources at www.napo.net/ or Professional Organizers Web Ring at www.organizerswebring.com.

3. Organizing Strategist (*Debbie Williams*) offers coaching, consulting, and an on-line forum for help organizing at www.organizedtimes.com. Her book, *Home Management 101: A Guide for Busy Parents* (Champion Press, 2001) is widely available. Visit her Web site at www.organizedtimes.com or call toll free 1-877-859-1585, or in Texas at 1-281-286-9512. You can also contact Debbie at info@organizedtimes.com.

4. Professional Organizer (*Barbara Hemphill*) offers consultants from www.thepapertiger.com and can be contacted at barbara@productiveenvironment.com or (919) 773-0722. Her books, *Taming the Paper Tiger at Home* and *Taming the Paper Tiger at Work* (both from Kiplinger, 1998) are excellent resources. The software, *Taming the Paper Tiger* provides a revolutionary new way to file and retrieve paper. The complete line of products can be found at www.productiveenvironment.com.

5. Professional Organizer (*Julie Morgenstern*) offers consultants from Taskmasters and can be contacted at organize@juliemorganstern.com or 1-86-ORGANISE (1-866-742-6473), or in New York at 1-212-544-8722. I also recommend her books, *Organizing From The Inside Out: The Foolproof System For Organizing Your Home, Your Office, And Your Life* (Owl Books, 1998) and *Time Management From The Inside Out: The Foolproof System For Taking Control Of Your Schedule—And Your Life* (Henry Holt, 2000). Also visit Morganstern's Web site www.juliemorganstern.com.

Mind and Spirit

> *You can be pleased with nothing when you are not pleased with yourself.*
>
> ~ *Lady Mary Wortley Montague*

TIP # 15 - REAFFIRM YOUR SENSE OF WORTH

Although your sense of worth is influenced by your interaction with others and by your experiences in the world, in the end, how you regard yourself is entirely up to you. Your perception of yourself becomes reality by the way you talk to yourself—your criticisms, whining, and negative self-talk. If any of the negativity is accurate, then why not get busy making changes so your self-worth improves. Allowing a negative core belief to take over is very damaging to your self-esteem. For instance, if you have labeled yourself as "lazy" or "disorganized" you tend to make that a reality in your explanations and justification of your own behavior. However, if you choose to control these behaviors, you can take actions to get organized and uncluttered and be a different kind of person, thus raising your own sense of worth.

Find as much as possible to appreciate in yourself as you do in others. Persistently encourage, rather than discourage yourself with limiting thoughts and behaviors. Make a conscious effort to take action rather than getting overwhelmed by fear and anxiety of what might happen. Don't let the excuses that justify behaviors prevent you from taking specific steps to achieve more successes.

The fact is, you can change the way you feel by changing the way you act. Eliminate the habits that lead to a negative self-image and, as a result, you can better manage the situations that leave you feeling down. Act "as if"—you're *already* successful, important, brave, or whatever you "wish" you were. By acting "as if" you are taking actions and behaving in a way that you would if it were already true today. Miraculously, perception becomes reality. In acting "as if" you

31

actually allow yourself to *become*. When you start acting in a manner that reaffirms your sense of worth, you'll rise in the estimation of someone important—YOU!

The gift of high self-esteem can also be passed on to your children. Imagine for a moment how your children's lives would be different without the critical inner voice and negative feelings that begin so early in life. By modeling a powerful self-worth, you can teach your kids how to be confident aspiring beings. You can help them take risks and be responsible for the actions they will take. Feelings are difficult to control or understand; behaviors are almost always controllable.

Related Activity: Answer the following (use the journal you started in Tip #1).

- What do you need to do right now to raise your self-esteem?
- What can you do tomorrow and the next day to continue improving your situation?
- What actions will bring you the success that will make you feel good about yourself?
- What do you keep putting off and avoiding?
- How would pushing through it increase your sense of worth?

Put aside your fears, nervousness, tension and anxieties, and just do it! Use someone in your personal or professional network, like a trusted friend or your coach, to provide some extra support and feedback to help you raise your self-esteem.

Recommended Resources

1. *A Women's Worth* by Marianne Williamson (Random House, Inc., 1994)
2. *Stand Up For Your Life: Develop The Courage, Confidence, And Character To Fulfill Your Greatest Potential* by Cheryl Richardson (Free Press, 2002)
3. *The Four Agreements: A Practical Guide To Personal Freedom* by Don Miguel Ruiz (Amber-Allen Publishing, 1999)

4. *Unlimited Power: The New Science Of Personal Achievement* by Anthony Robbins (Fireside, 1997)
5. *What To Say When You Talk To Your Self* by Shad Helmstetter (Pocket Books, 1987)

Be Proud of WHO You Are!

I think that, as life is action and passion, it is required of a man that he should share the passion and action of his time at peril of being judged not to have lived.

~ MacIver

Tip # 16 - Determine Your Passion

Working parents often struggle with work and personal life balance issues. To help you balance the time you devote to your personal and professional life, determine your passion. What truly ignites you and inspires you? What do you absolutely love doing? Where are your natural gifts and talents? How could you earn a living doing something you are absolutely passionate about?

Too often your own beliefs are limiting and preventing you from allocating time to both your personal and professional life. Are you making decisions and taking actions based on what you "should" be doing, "ought" to be doing, or what you "have to do?" If so, these external drivers (see Tip #1) are not as effective as the internal sources of direction such as your values, priorities, or needs (see Tips #18 and #20).

Related Activity: Begin replacing the "should's," "ought's," and "have to's" in your life with "I want," "I choose," and "I prefer." Realize that you are in control of your own life and everything is really about choice, including choosing not to do anything! Up until now your life choices have determined who you are and where you are. Take control!

Recommended Resources

1. *Finding Your Passion* by Cheryl Richardson (audiotape by Hay House, Inc., 2002)
2. *Live With Passion! Create A Compelling Future With America's Top Business And Life Strategist* by Anthony Robbins (compact disc by Simon & Schuster Audio, 2002)
3. *The Impossible Just Takes A Little Longer: Lessons On Living With Purpose And Passion* by Art Berg (William Morrow & Company, 2002)

For today and its blessings, I owe the world an attitude of gratitude.
                                                              ~ Clarance Hodges

TIP # 17 - LIVE WITH THE ATTITUDE OF GRATITUDE

Giving thanks comes in many forms, but it always comes from inside...from your heart and from a place of abundance and gratitude. Adapting the attitude of gratitude will help you get by on even the roughest of days. Living in gratitude helps you focus on what you have to be thankful for and helps you look on the brighter side of things.

Begin consciously enjoying the little things in life and stop acting on autopilot. Take time to be introspective and to offer thanks for freedom and family. At home and at work, surround yourself with reminders of what you are most thankful for. It's so easy to get caught up in the daily stresses and to lose perspective about what's most important to you. Living in gratitude helps you to live in the moment, be fully present, and connected with who and what's around you.

Adapting an attitude of gratitude gives you the opportunity to change your experiences. Gratitude is a state of *being* not just a momentary feeling. Look at the things in your own life that are causing you feelings of stress, sadness or anger (like you or your spouse getting laid off); *consciously choose* to change the experience by looking at those types of situations with a new perspective (i.e., it's an opportunity for a new beginning at another company, to return to school, or to spend more time with family).

You can control your feelings, attitude, and behavior in any situation. You can focus on what you have to be grateful for, especially in times when things don't feel like they are going well. In many cases, you can't change the situation; however, you can change how you choose to feel about it, how you allow the situation to affect you, and how you respond to it. Being in gratitude helps you remain calmer in a crisis. It helps you accept things that may be difficult to accept. It also helps you keep a positive mood while feeling more centered and balanced. When you go through your day in a state of gratitude, it's almost impossible to feel down.

Although things may look bleak and hopeless at times, think about what you have to be grateful for today. Even in situations that seem far from perfect, there are valuable lessons to learn, relationships to cherish, and probably numerous reasons to be thankful. Look for those things...cherish and appreciate them.

You can demonstrate gratitude in words and/or actions. For instance, when you bring in breakfast or lunch for your co-workers you are expressing your appreciation to them. When you donate money or items to charity you are helping others who may be less fortunate. And when you volunteer your time and services you are demonstrating a commitment to supporting others.

Your children learn largely by observing you. Model those behaviors and actions you would like to see in them. Involve them in age-appropriate ways and help them find ways to express their own gratitude.

Related Activity: Share the spirit of goodwill by expressing heartfelt gratitude for the blessings in your life. Make a list of 10 things/people you are thankful for. Tell those people why you are grateful for them and/or share with someone close the things you are grateful for.

Recommended Resources

1. *Attitudes Of Gratitude: How To Give And Receive Joy Every Day Of Your Life* by M.J. Ryan (Conari Press, 2000)
2. *Gratitude: Affirming The Good Things In Life* by Melody Beattie (Fine Communications, 1999)
3. *The Simple Abundance Journal Of Gratitude* by Sarah Ban Breathnach (Warner Books, Inc., 1996)

> *Know thyself.*
>
> *~ Socrates*

TIP # 18 - RE-ORIENT YOUR LIFE AROUND YOUR VALUES

Values are those traits that are nearest and dearest to you. They are at the core of *who* you are; they are your heart and soul. When you are engaged in activities aligned with your values, you feel most like yourself: well, connected, excited, glowing, and effortless. However, when what you are doing conflicts with what is truly important to you, feelings of unhappiness, dissatisfaction, frustration, and stress occur most often because your values conflict with your lifestyle. This discord can get so out of tune that it can literally become unhealthy.

Values are what you are naturally inclined, drawn to, or eager to do, without much effort or even goal setting. They run deep within you and are often disguised when danger is sensed. Danger in this case is anything that may interfere with or intrude on your values, such as: needs, obligations, roles, problems, should's, addictions, or adrenaline.

Living a values-based life brings fulfillment—that inner feeling (beyond happiness or satisfaction) of being totally you. Life is simpler, richer, and with fewer distractions. Discovering and clarifying your values will guide you through the decision paths in your life. When you live life based on your values, you live with a unique and blended harmony.

Related Activity: Determine your key values by asking yourself: *What is really most important to me in my life?* Extract your core values based on what is most important to you, your actions, and the things you choose to do and not do in your life. The activities you engage in are a demonstration of your values; the values themselves are intangible. In some cases, I have my clients use a checklist to identify their values. Another way to clarify your values is to extract them from your life by examining where they show up, which are most immutable, and which are sometimes neglected. A helpful exercise is to create a list of your 10 most important values and then rank order the list from the most important on down. The real value from this exercise comes from the thought process involved with evaluating one value against another to rank order them and not from the list itself. The examination forces you to choose one value over another, thus having you think about the importance of each in your life.

Then examine where you are in your life and see how closely your current choices reflect those values. *How are you honoring your values?* You might find it a bit uncomfortable as you notice that some of your choices have pulled you farther away from your values. Use this information to begin to make changes and new choices...to get your life aligned with what *is* most important to you.

Recommended Resources

1. *Emotional Intelligence* by Daniel Goldman (Bantam Books Inc., 1997)
2. *In Search of Values: 31 Strategies For Finding Out What Really Matters Most To You* by Sidney B. Simon (Warner Books, 1993)
3. *Values Clarification: The Classic Guide To Discovering Your Truest Feelings* by Sidney B. Simon (Warner Books, 1995)
4. *What Matters Most: The Power Of Living Your Values* by Hyrum W. Smith with foreword by Ken Blanchard (Simon & Schuster, 2001)

> *Your only obligation in any lifetime is to be true to yourself.*
> ~ *Richard Bach*

TIP # 19 - CREATE CLEAR BOUNDARIES

Boundaries are imaginary lines that help you protect yourself both physically and emotionally. They keep other's actions and behaviors from hurting, distracting, annoying, or imposing on you. Setting stronger boundaries will help you stand up for yourself, stop agreeing to do things you really don't want to do, and start feeling less guilty about putting your own needs first. When you don't have boundaries set other people will step over the line without even realizing where it is. You often wind up saying "yes" to things you don't want to do and end up feeling angry, frustrated, and resentful.

Having strong boundaries are important if you're going to protect your body, mind, and spirit. The first step in setting better boundaries is self-awareness; you'll need to identify where you need more space, self-respect, energy, and/or personal power. Begin this process by recognizing when you feel angry, frustrated, violated, or resentful. In these cases, you've often had a boundary "broken." By becoming aware of situations that require you to have stronger limits, you can begin creating and communicating your new boundaries to others.

Creating boundaries at work and home will help you honor yourself more. It's perfectly okay to request or demand respect from others and to honor yourself. Someone's tone of voice, negativity, criticism, derogatory language, or other form of disrespect, may prompt you to create a boundary in order to protect yourself and your goals from disruptive influences. Give yourself permission to begin honoring yourself and others in new ways. Boundaries are an important way for you to respect the needs of others, as well as your own. Ironically, when you become aware of your boundaries (and begin to respect them) you'll naturally begin to regard the boundaries of others, as well.

It's important to note that in establishing boundaries:

- Your personal needs are valid. It is not necessary for you to defend, debate or over-explain your request.
- Enlist the support of a friend for before and after the boundary-setting conversation, if necessary.
- Begin setting boundaries with the easiest ones and build yourself up to the more challenging ones for you. Let your communication and behavior get stronger before you tackle the harder boundaries.
- Tell people immediately when they are doing something that violates one of your boundaries.
- Simply tell them what they are doing that makes you feel angry, frustrated, violated, resentful, or uncomfortable. Communicate gracefully and honestly.
- Make a direct request that they stop the behaviors that offend or bother you.
- Inform them about the change you need to see.
- Thank them for making the change.

And, if they refuse to cooperate:

- Demand that they stop, or
- Just walk away without getting angry or fighting.

Over time and with practice, setting boundaries will get easier. Remember that it's a way to fully honor and respect yourself. You can control your own response by delivering your request gracefully to the other person, but you can't control the other person's response or behavior to your request. People who continuously refuse to respect and honor your boundaries are clearly not willing to change. The change you need to see may come from yourself. Be sure that you have provided direct requests and communicated your boundaries consistently. If you have, and they still refuse to honor your boundary, it's up to you to decide how you wish to proceed. In these (hopefully rare) cases, you may need to negotiate further or end the relationship.

Related Activity: Complete the following statements:

People may no longer...
I have a right to ask for...
To protect my time and energy, it's okay to...

Then, finish each sentence with at least 12 examples (or more) of boundaries you can set to honor yourself. Don't censor your thoughts. Keep jotting down ideas over the course of the next week or so. Then, select the easiest ones and start communicating your boundaries.

Recommended Resources

1. *Boundaries: When To Say Yes, When To Say No To Take Control Of Your Life* by Henry Cloud and John Townsend (Zondervan Publishing House, 2002)
2. *Parents In Charge: Setting Healthy, Loving Boundaries For You And Your Child* by Dane Chidekel (Simon & Schuster, 2002)
3. *Where To Draw The Line: How To Set Up Healthy Boundaries Everyday* by Anne Katherine (Simon & Schuster, 2000)
4. *Working Parent—Happy Child* by Caryl Waller Krueger (Nashville/ Abingdon Press, 1990)

> *What I do today is important because I am exchanging a day of my life for it.*
>
> ~ *Hugh Mulligan*

TIP # 20 - LIVE BY YOUR PRIORITIES

One of the keys to a happier life is to organize and execute your life based on your priorities. When you focus on your *priorities* you're better able to *consciously decide* how to spend your time and attention.

I often have clients do an exercise that is adapted from Cheryl Richardson's book, *Take Time for Your Life*. She calls it an "Absolute Yes" list. This list contains your top 5–7 priorities for right now. When I did this exercise with one of my clients, who's a full-time professor and a single mom, she wrote her "Absolute Yes" items on easel paper in her office and on a 3x5 card she carried along with her. She referenced her list often so that she didn't over-commit or agree to do anything that would take her away from her real priorities. One of her priorities was to create a loving and peaceful home for her and her sons during and after her divorce. She consciously made decisions using her priority list as her guidance. She did not ridicule her ex-husband in front of the kids; she created specific visitation arrangements; she sold her home and moved across town to a smaller more manageable home that the boys helped her select; and she organized her new home using the principles of Feng Shui (the Chinese art and science that explores our relationship to our surroundings to promote health and prosperity).

This client's decisions were in alignment with her values, needs, and goals. When you live your life based on your priorities, knowing what's most important to you and giving it your full attention, your life is integrated. On the other hand, when you spend your time on the things that are simply urgent or unimportant, you are distracted from what truly matters and you often end up feeling frustrated and angry. Recognizing your priorities and living your life based on them will lead to a happier life.

Related Activity: Realize that you have a choice about how you live your life and spend your time each day. If you're not living your life based on your priorities, you can either continue operating in the same manner hoping that things will improve, or you can take control of your life—do something about it! Complete the following exercise:

1. Record how you use your time over the course of the next week; become aware of the activities that comprise your average day. Without going crazy with details, calculate the time you spend on *work-related activities* (i.e., working, commuting, preparing for work, worrying about work-related problems); *family-related activities* (i.e., schlepping the kids to their activities, preparing meals, shopping for groceries, doing household chores, having meals together, caring for the kids, "dating" your spouse); and *activities for you* (i.e., sleeping, exercising, personal hygiene, reading, meditating).

2. Create a list of your current priorities based on how your time is being spent right now. *What 5–7 activities are getting the majority of your time and attention?*

3. Analyze your list to determine where your life is balanced, what you want more or less of. Ask yourself: *Are these really my priorities? Am I spending my time on the things that I say are most important to me?*

4. Now, take some time to develop a new list of priorities based on what *is* really important to you. Consider the areas that need more attention and those you want to spend less time on. Choose priorities that are personally important to you from each main area of your life (i.e., your personal well-being and health, relationships, family, finances, physical environment, career).

5. Begin living your life based on these priorities. Look for ways to honor your priorities within the context of your everyday life rather than trying to add more to your already full plate. Re-orient your life around what is most important to you!

Recommended Resources

1. *First Things First: To Live, To Love, To Learn, To Leave A Legacy* by Stephen Covey (Simon & Schuster, 1995)
2. *Move Your Stuff, Change Your Life: How To Use Feng Shui To Get Love, Money, Respect, And Happiness* by Karen Rauch Carter (Simon & Schuster, 1999)
3. *Take Time For Your Life: A Personal Coach's 7-Step Program For Creating The Life You Want* by Cheryl Richardson (Broadway Books, 1998)
4. *The Seven Habits Of Highly Effective People* by Stephen Covey (Simon & Shuster, 1990)

What Matters Most to You?

Personal Growth and Development

TIP # 21 - SIMPLY SAY "NO"

As a parent, you often say "yes" when you want to say "no" because you want to be liked, you want to help, be needed, or avoid disappointing or hurting others. Demands on your time, services, and resources come in on an almost daily basis. Often you respond and commit to doing *something* because you feel guilty for not spending enough time with your children. However, simply saying "yes" or agreeing to something because it seems easier (or you wouldn't dare say "no") diminishes you. When you say "yes" too often you do so begrudgingly.

You always have the right to turn down a request. The inability to say "no" is one of the main obstacles that prevent most people from living the lives they want. It's easier than you think to say "no" in a nice but direct way. Try out some of these examples:

- I know someone else who can...
- Sorry, I'm already booked...
- We have a family commitment...
- I've decided/chosen not to...
- No, thank you...
- No, I don't want to...

Before you respond be clear on what the person is asking and realize you don't have to justify your reason for saying "no." Just be firm, clear, brief, and to the point when you decline. Be sure that your body language is giving the same message as your words. There is no need to feel guilty or apologetic about your "no"; you have the right to say "no." If you want to make a compromise, then let the requester know what you are willing to do. You only need to do what you want to do!

For example, while I was writing this book I became interested in some local issues that had an impact on my family. When I talked with the mayor about my concerns, he invited me to participate in (or lead) a committee to fully address the issues. I was flattered and may have ordinarily eagerly said "yes." However, knowing that I was already committed to spending quality time with my family, running my business, serving my clients, and writing this book, I knew I didn't have the time to devote to that work. I politely turned him down and thanked him for the offer to work on the committee.

Related Activity: Ask yourself: *"If I could say "no" to someone or something, knowing that there would be absolutely no hard feelings or negative consequences, who or what would I say "no" to?"* Make a list of at least five things you would say "no" to based on this question. Beginning with the first "no" on your list, take action to reverse the yes's, or communicate the no's more effectively. It's okay to say no or to change your mind, especially when you're feeling overwhelmed or pressed for time. The next time someone makes a request of you (whether at work or at home), put some space between their request and your response rather than responding automatically, say "I'll get back to you on that." Practice, practice, practice...it *will* get easier!

Recommended Resources

1. *201 Ways To Say No Effectively And Gracefully* by Alan Axelrod (McGraw Hill Trade, 1997)
2. *Don't Say Yes When You Want To Say No* by Herbert Fensterheim with Jean Baer (Dell Books, 1975)
3. *How To Say No Without Feeling Guilty: And Say Yes To More Time, More Joy, And What Matters Most To You* by Patti Breitman (Broadway Books, 2001)
4. *Learning To Say No: Establishing Healthy Boundaries* by Carla Wills Brandon (ToExcel, 2000)

5. *When I Say No, I Feel Guilty* by Manuel J. Smith (Bantam Books, 1975)
6. *Your Perfect Right: Assertiveness And Equality In Your Life And Relationships* by Robert E. Alberti & Michael L. Emmons (Impact Publishers Inc., 2001)

Just Say "NO"!

> *You don't have to control your thoughts, you just have to stop letting them control you.*
>
> *~ Dan Millman*

TIP # 22 - LET GO OF GUILT

Guilt is one of the greatest wastes of emotional energy. It may cause you to become immobilized and it can be very debilitating. By introducing logic to help counter-balance the guilt, you can better stay on course.

So, what is guilt?

- Guilt is the knowledge that what you have done is not right, that you are personally responsible for this action, and will ultimately be held accountable.
- Guilt is a condition and not a feeling. Using guilt as a feeling masks deeper emotions and the identity of the real problem.
- Guilt is something that naturally transcends the entire human race because we all have a conscience.

There are basically two types of *guilt*:

Productive (good) guilt: Causes you to move forward (e.g., contemplating other options, comparing choices to your values) and gets you away from destructive behavior. It includes being flexible and willing to make other choices. Some examples of what comes from productive guilt include forgiveness, confessions to something that needs to be aired, making choices, and planning activities together. For example, when you're feeling guilty for not spending enough time with your kids, plan an activity rather than just feeling badly about it.

Remorseful (bad/nonproductive) guilt: Is destructive and paralyzing. It's when you don't allow logic in to reject the guilt you are experiencing. It includes those times when you keep beating yourself up for something you did (or didn't do), and when you are stuck and unable to do anything. Immobilization, being totally pre-occupied, and perfectionism may be a result of remorseful guilt.

Related Activity: Take a close look at why you feel guilty and work toward resolving the problem versus a symptom. Take some time to identify the real problem. Then, develop 10 affirmations to support the choices that you've made, like "I am where I need to be," "My children are being well cared for in my absence." Do something about what you are feeling guilty over rather than consuming yourself with guilt that is nonproductive.

Recommended Resources

1. *A Mother's Place: Choosing Work And Family Without Guilt Or Blame* by Susan Chira (Harper Collins, 1999)
2. *When Mothers Work: Loving Our Children Without Sacrificing Ourselves* by Joan K. Peters (Perseus Publishing, 1998)

> *When you love the people you are speaking to, loving them with awareness and skillfulness, and when you also tell the truth, they will nearly always gladly receive whatever you have to say.*
>
> ~ *Author Unknown*

TIP # 23 - SAY WHAT YOU MEAN

Communication between people can be very complicated, especially when they don't always say what they really mean. By being up-front and clear during the conversation, you'll have a better opportunity to truly connect and support one other.

There are many reasons that people don't communicate what they really want to say. Often, they're afraid of conflict or of hurting someone's feelings. The truth is, you can *grow through conflict* and *deepen your relationships* with others by *working through the challenges.* By avoiding conflict or confrontation, you eliminate the possibility of connecting on a deeper level.

You can't hurt someone's feelings unless that person chooses to allow that to happen. You can't control how the other person will choose to react, but you can control how you communicate. In relationships, if you are trying to second-guess how you're going to say something, you're doing the relationship a disservice. Come from a place of love and generosity and have integrity about what you're saying. Say what you mean for the sake of a true honest relationship. Be sincere and loving even in your criticisms. You don't need to make someone wrong in order to communicate honestly.

For instance, a client of mine was struggling over some issues in one of her long-term friendships. She was feeling very annoyed because the friend didn't return her phone calls and often cancelled plans at the last minute. Rather than calling her friend and berating her for not calling, she sent her friend a lovely note that expressed what she was feeling and how important the friendship is to her. Her friend called to apologize and explained the reasons for cancelling and not returning phone calls, and made (and kept) a date for the next week.

Related Activity: Be clear and honest in your communications with others. It will help strengthen your connections and relationships. If you say what you mean, you won't have to worry about whether the other person has gotten your message, or hope that the other person is a mind reader. Practice what you need to say before saying it when you have something that you are holding back and not fully expressing. Get into the habit of communicating with love and truthfulness in all your relationships.

Recommended Resources

1. *How To Communicate: The Ultimate Guide To Improving Your Personal And Professional Relationships* by Davis McKay (Fine Communications, 1997)
2. *Say What You Mean, Mean What You Say: 10 Surefire Ways To Get The Results You Want* by Cheryl Cran (Trafford Publishing, 2001)
3. *The Art Of Talking So That People Will Listen: Getting Through To Family, Friends, And Business Associates* by Paul W. Swets (Simon & Schuster, 1992)

> *Deep listening is miraculous for both listener and speaker. When someone receives us with open-hearted, non-judging, intensely interested listening, our spirits expand.*
>
> *~ Sue Patton Thoele*

TIP # 24 - LISTEN WITH YOUR EARS, EYES, AND HEART

To truly connect with the people around you, you must listen attentively to what they are saying. However, we often "hear" instead of *listen* while engaged in conversations with others. Listening well occurs when you stop talking and stop simply waiting for your opportunity to jump in to respond to what you've heard. When you listen fully, you listen with your whole body and heart so you not only hear what the other person is saying, but what you feel. You'll also tend to hear what they're *not* saying—you'll be sort of, "listening between the lines"—listening to changes in their tone, speed, and other expressions both verbally and nonverbally.

Put the talker at ease and show her that you truly want to listen to what she has to say. Improved listening will take time, practice, focus, and patience. When you truly listen, you create an energetic connection between you and the person you are listening to; an invisible tie connects you and allows you to see deep into the other person and get a better understanding of who he is.

Listening helps you learn more about others and yourself. It also helps others feel valued and respected. Make the time to listen attentively and look for nonverbal clues, as well.

Related Activity: Go on a listening mission. Listen keenly to what others say (or don't say). Focus your attention directly on them. Key into their voice, tone, body language, and facial expressions. Feel the connection you have with that person. Keep practicing so that it begins to become natural to truly listen to your kids, spouse, work colleagues, friends, and others.

Recommended Resources

1. *Listen Up: How To Improve Relationships, Reduce Stress, And Be More Productive By Using The Power Of Listening* by Larry Lee (St. Martin's Press, 2000)
2. *Listening: The Forgotten Skill (A Self-Teaching Guide)* by Madelyn Burley-Allen (John Wiley & Sons, 1995)

Success for Super Busy Parents

Key Essential #4

TWO-WAY COMMUNICATION

Communication involves speaking and listening. Be aware of what you need and be prepared to ask for it. Establish & communicate boundaries that honor you. Be fully engaged in conversations so that you hear what others are *really* saying.

> *The main reason people struggle financially is because they have spent years in school but learned nothing about money. The result is that people learn to work for money but never learn to have money work for them.*
>
> *~ Robert Kiyosaki*

TIP # 25 - GAIN FINANCIAL FREEDOM

Financial freedom means that you have more than enough money to live on now, and enough to support your family for the rest of your life. It comes when you are free of financial concerns as you manage your money. From this place, your choices and goals are not influenced by the making of money. You are who you want to be, you do what you want to do, and you're happy.

The fact is, financial freedom is possible for everyone. It may require radical and immediate action to get on track and stay on track to attain your financial goals. It may take the commitment of everyone in your family to establish a budget and stay within it on a regular basis. Although money can't necessarily bring happiness, the lack of it can bring plenty of misery and pain. In order to be in control of your life, you need to establish financial reserves.

The result of financial freedom is that it provides opportunity for you to make decisions that you wouldn't otherwise feel you have.

Related Activity: Analyze your financial situation and determine exactly where you are out of financial integrity. Use a professional advisor, debt counselor or other financial expert, if necessary. Create a workable plan that enables you to make some long-range goals while beginning to tackle some things immediately. Start with your highest priorities and get into action today! You must begin with a solid plan in order to restore financial integrity. Enlist the help and support of those around you to provide an extra level of accountability.

Recommended Resources

1. *Cashflow Quadrant: Rich Dad's Guide To Financial Freedom* by Robert Kiyosaki and Sharon L. Lechter (Warner Business Books, 2000)
2. *Making Money, Creating Wealth: Your Guide To Financial Independence* by Philip C. Humbert, PhD (download free at www.philiphumbert.com/eBook.htm)
3. *Nine Steps To Financial Freedom: Practical And Spiritual Steps So You Can Stop Worrying* by Suze Orman (Crowne Publishers, Inc., 1997)
4. *Rich Dad, Poor Dad: What The Rich Teach Their Kids About Money—That The Poor And Middle Class Do Not!* by Robert T. Kiyosaki and Sharon L. Lechter (Warner Business Books, 2000)
5. *Financial Guidebook: Put The 9 Steps To Work* by Suze Orman (Three Rivers Press, 2002)
6. *Your Money Or Your Life: Transforming Your Relationship With Money And Achieving Financial Independence* by Joe Dominguez (Penguin USA, 1999)

Manage Your Finances!

Part 2

BALANCE YOUR FAMILY LIFE

Parenting

TIP # 26 - BE FULLY PRESENT AND FOCUSED

Have your kids ever told you that you weren't really paying attention to them because you were obviously engaged in something else at the time? Have your co-workers ever fought to get your attention? Has your boss requested something from you, only to get something else in return? These are all examples of situations where, although you were there when someone else was talking to you, in effect you weren't really there.

Society has conditioned us to continually multitask (doing several activities simultaneously, see Tip #72). By focusing fully on one person, project, or activity you are better able to maximize your creativity and be more responsive to others.

Most people wear multiple hats at any given time. Many of us are pursuing financial independence, want to spend more time with our family and friends, want to take better care of ourselves, and contribute more to society. But you can't focus on all of these things simultaneously. By focusing on what you are doing at any given time, you allow yourself to get absorbed in the activity, be more relaxed, and increase your creativity. The objective is to focus on what you're engaged in doing at the moment. According to Zig Zigler, motivational speaker and author, "To be successful in life, you need to learn to work toward one major objective and juggle two to three short-range to mid-range goals at a time."

Working parents frequently feel they don't have enough time with their families, or that the time spent with them is too frantic. You do have a choice about how you live your life and how you spend your time. Be deliberate in how you use your time.

Related Activity: For a week, select at least 30 minutes each day when you will fully listen to your children. During this time, stop everything else you are doing, thinking or saying and put your full attention on your child. Rather than reacting immediately to what you hear, respond thoughtfully.

Also, practice the technique of *mirroring* with your children to adapt your communication style to theirs. Mirroring is a communication tool that helps you establish rapport with another person in a respectful way. It is based on the assumption that we tend to feel comfortable with people who communicate nonverbally in a similar way to ourselves. It is the practice of duplicating words and postures exhibited by others as a way to build rapport.

During mirroring you physically copy (not *mimic* or *imitate*) what your child is doing for a few moments without being distracting or annoying. You follow and interpret their body language, voice speed, and tone so that you speak slowly when they speak slowly, speak softly when they speak softly, and you lean forward when they lean forward. In other words, you get in synch with them by mirroring their tone of voice and body language during the initial stages of the conversation. (This technique also works well with other people!)

Recommended Resources

1. *How To Talk So Kids Will Listen & Listen So Kids Will Talk* by Adele Faber and Elaine Mazlish (Avon Books, 1999)
2. *Successful Child: What Parents Can Do To Help Kids Turn Out Well* by William and Martha Sears (Little Brown & Company, 2002)
3. *The Seven Habits of Highly Effective Families: Building A Beautiful Family Culture In A Turbulent World* by Stephen R. Covey (Golden Books, 1997)

> *Success and leadership demand that you make tough, important and even controversial decisions—often in advance—if you expect to reach your full potential.*
>
> ~ Zig Zigler

TIP # 27 - DECIDE WHERE YOU NEED TO BE

Sometimes, when your children are involved in multiple activities like sports, hobbies, or clubs you may need to sacrifice what you want to do for (or with) your family at the moment for their long-term benefit. Although other factors may often affect your decision, this tip will focus mainly on the financial considerations.

For example, choosing to be at an activity at a time when you're facing financial challenges may not be using your best judgment. The financial rewards may be so great that your family would best be served in the long-run by making the decision a financial one. When you're on the verge of closing a substantial sale, getting a well-deserved promotion, or other sought after opportunity, don't lose sight of the fact that your long-range responsibilities are to provide for your family. You're not actually serving them by choosing to leave your work responsibilities in these situations.

On the other hand, if you're usually deciding in favor of work rather than family obligations, the long-term price on your family is far too high. Be aware of how often you choose business over family. If the financial considerations start winning over more regularly, then sometimes you may opt to choose your family regardless of possible financial gains. Much can be said about the value of parents being at every game, event, or performance of their children; however you can make conscious choices from time-to-time about what's in your overall best interest.

Use your judgment and be honest with your family when telling them about your other obligations on the occasions when you can't make an event. Making balanced decisions will help you have a more balanced life. If your financial difficulties are severe, seek help and work toward financial freedom (see Tip #25).

Related Activity: This week, make a conscious choice about where you need to be. Be wherever you choose 100% and don't dwell on your decision or what you should've, could've, or would've done.

Recommended Resources

1. *Busy But Balanced: Practical And Inspirational Ways To Create A Calmer, Closer Family* by Mimi Doe (St. Martin's Press, 2001)
2. *Josh McDowell's One Year Book Of Family Devotions* by Josh McDowell (Tyndale House Publishers, 1997)
3. *Putting Family First: Successful Strategies For Reclaiming Family Life In A Hurry-Up World* by William J. Doherty and Barbara Z. Carlson (Henry Holt & Company Inc., 2002)
4. *Success for Dummies* by Zig Zigler (IDG Books Worldwide, 1998)

Be Where You Need To Be!

> *Parents can only give good advice or put one on the right paths, but the final forming of a person's character lies in their own hands.*
>
> ~ *Anne Frank*

TIP # 28 - PRACTICE "PEACEFUL PARENTING"

I had the distinct pleasure of meeting Naomi Drew, author of *Peaceful Parents, Peaceful Kids: Practical Ways to Create a Calm and Happy Home*. In her book, Drew writes about key essentials for parenting peacefully. As a working parent, your time and patience may be more limited than others; however, these principles are worth implementing in your home.

Key Essential #1: Catch your children in the act of doing things *right* and sincerely commend them immediately. Be specific so that they understand your praise. Your kids basically want to please you. When you acknowledge the positive things they do, you hold up a mirror to their best selves and help them see the behaviors you want them to replicate. Kids want to recapture the positive feelings they have when you recognize their good behaviors, so they tend to repeat the things that were the sources of praise.

Key Essential #2: Eliminate put-downs. Put-downs destroy self-esteem and teach children the habit of putting others down. Resist the impulse to use criticism, negative labels, sarcasm, or comparisons. This applies to every member of your family. Commit to making your home a put-down free zone.

Key Essential #3: Spend at least 15–20 minutes a day of uninterrupted time with each child. One of the main reasons that kids act out is because they want your time and attention. Use preventative medicine. By giving each child a small block of time on a regular basis, you send a vital message: "You're important." During your 15–20 minutes, be with your child and completely listen to what he has to say. You can do jobs together like folding laundry or drying dishes, but be with your child exclusively and focus your full attention on her. Your relationship with your child will become much more peaceful as a result.

Although I've touched upon these key points elsewhere in this book, I thought it would be useful to reiterate them together here because they are some of the core essentials to parenting peacefully. Drew also wrote *The Peaceful Classroom in Action* and *Learning the Skills of Peacemaking* as resources for K-6 educators. Her latest book is *Hope and Healing: Peaceful Parenting in an Uncertain World*.

Visit www.learningpeace.com for more information about Naomi Drew and for help with teaching your kids the concrete skills they need to get along well with others.

Related Activity: Choose any one of the essentials from above and implement it immediately. If you're already doing all of them—bravo! Evaluate how well your tactics are working and how much peace you have in your home. If adjustments are necessary, do them so that you have more peace and joy in your home.

Recommended Resource

Peaceful Parents, Peaceful Kids: Practical Ways To Create A Calm And Happy Home by Naomi Drew (New York/Kensington Books, 2000)

> *A baby is born with a need to be loved and never outgrows it.*
>
> ~ *Frank A. Clark*

TIP # 29 - FIND HIGH-QUALITY CHILD CARE

There are a number of options available when selecting the childcare that best suits the needs of you, your children, and your family. To determine what's best, it's important to consider their disposition, your work hours, your needs, and your comfort level in each situation. Be open-minded when researching and evaluating your options. Seek recommendations from other parents you know and trust.

Finding the best, safest, and most educational childcare is anything but easy. You must think through your decisions and look at all the available resources before you make your final decision. Once you've identified some childcare possibilities, conduct telephone interviews to screen places and narrow down your list. Ask a lot of questions, especially about the things that are most important to you (e.g., experience and background of the caregivers, the environment, or number of other children being cared for).

According to recent studies about the quality of childcare (at daycare centers), the most important indicators of high-quality childcare are related directly to the teachers or caregivers. For example, the education and training of staff, the number of children for whom the teacher or caregiver is responsible (staff-to-child ratio), the ability of staff to build relationships with parents, and the capacity of staff to develop a child-centered program in a stimulating environment are all interrelated indicators of quality.

Visit each selected provider or center, observe the interactions and environment, and ask any questions you have. Request the contact information for at least three legitimate references and call them to discuss what they like and don't like about their childcare. Although it's not a guarantee that the center will be right for you, when considering daycare centers, look for accreditation and independent seals of approval that designate that the facility has undergone rigorous analysis and maintains minimum standards.

Being comfortable with your childcare arrangement is critical for every working parent. When you feel that your child is being loved and well cared for in your absence you will have more peace of mind. The more information you have about the caregiver, the program, the rules, cost, and environment the more confident you will feel in making your decision. It's hard enough parting with your child; make sure you are placing him in good hands. Even after you've done all your research, asked your questions, and chosen what you believe to be the best care for your child, continue to evaluate your child's progress and comfort. Pop in unannounced every now and then to observe your child and the care he is receiving.

Here are some basic pros and cons to consider when exploring your childcare options:

Daycare Center	
PROS	CONS
• Provides a structured program in a licensed environment.	• May lead to more illnesses for your child due to exposure to more children.
• Often one of the least expensive options.	• May offer less individualized attention.
• Exposes child to a diverse group of children and providers.	• Pay a flat monthly rate regardless of whether or not your child attends.
• Since the center is usually open (except on weekends and holidays), you will not need to find back-up care if a provider becomes ill.	• Must make other arrangements when the center closes for holidays and snow days.
• Easier to schedule part-time care.	• Specific hours for opening and closing times with stiff penalties for late pick-up.
	• Often has a high turnover rate of caregivers.

Family Care

PROS	CONS
• Provides home environment and playmates that are usually of varying ages. • Offers exposure to a smaller number of children and, therefore, less exposure to illness. • May be more individualized and nurturing care. • May offer more flexible hours.	• Not many family childcare homes are licensed. • Difficult to monitor quality of care. • Requires good backup plan if provider becomes ill.

Family Members

PROS	CONS
• Care is provided by a close friend or member of your family. • Sometimes you and your partner can scatter your work hours so that the two of you are the primary care givers. • Low-cost (or no cost) flexible and secure childcare.	• Informal arrangement with friends or relatives. • Often difficult to discuss issues that arise. • May be tough on your relationship with your partner because you seldom spend time together when you work shift schedules.

AuPair

PROS	CONS
• Usually a foreign national lives in your home while she provides childcare and does some housework. • Trained in childcare or have cared for their siblings. • Often more affordable than other options because you are providing room and board. • Flexible hours.	• Possible language barriers. • Another (child) to be responsible for because this young adult is living with you. • Many agencies suggest using only for older children or when the parent is also in the home during the day.

In-Home Private Babysitter or Nanny

PROS	CONS
• Provides one-on-one care that may be more nurturing.	• Need strong backup plan when provider is ill.
• Easier than transporting child to and from a facility.	• Less social stimulation for child.
• Child stays in comfortable, familiar home environment.	• Usually the most expensive option.
• Less exposure to illnesses.	• Difficult to monitor quality of care.
• Often helps with other responsibilities such as light housekeeping for children's needs, shopping, and preparing meals.	

Family Co-op

PROS	CONS
• A number of families group together to arrange or hire childcare.	• Your kids are sometimes bounced around between homes of co-op members.
• Works well when families are working in part-time or job share arrangements.	• You're coordinating details and doing a lot of the scheduling yourself.
• Costs are sometimes significantly lower than some of the other options.	• You may end up having more kids to care for than just your own on your days off.
• Your kids get to play with a small group of other children on a fairly consistent basis.	

Before/After Care:

PROS	CONS
• Childcare is provided for school-age children before and/or after regular school hours.	• Makes for a long day for the kids.
• Sometimes provided right at the school your child attends.	• Sometimes prevents your children from participating in other activities of interest.

Related Activity: Take your time when choosing the right childcare for you and your child. Carefully consider the options. After visiting several programs, close your eyes and try to imagine your child spending most of their waking hours in each of the settings. Which one do you feel best about? Trust your instincts! (Note: If you are pregnant and will be returning to work quickly, start looking for high-quality childcare now. Waiting lists for infant care can be long.)

Recommended Resources

1. *How To Find The Best Quality Child Care* by Michael J. Matthews (Autumn Publishing Group, 1998)
2. *Nannies, Au Pairs* And *Babysitters: How To Find And Keep The Right In-Home Childcare For Your Family* by Jerri L. Wolfe, Editor of Redbook Magazine (Hearst Books, 2001)
3. *The Anxious Parents' Guide To Quality Childcare: An Informative, Step-by-Step Manual On Finding And Keeping The Finest Care For Your Child* by Michelle Ehrich (Berkley Publishing Group, 1999)

> *It is not a parent's job to protect their kids from life, but to prepare them for it.*
>
> *~ Blake Segal*

TIP # 30 - TRANSITION TO AT-HOME PARENTING

If you are one of the many parents who have decided to leave your career to raise your family, this tip will help you ease the transition. At-home parents embrace a life enriched with numerous rewards and challenges. However, the transition can be rough when you are accustomed to devoting much of your life to your work.

One of the most important things for you to do is to allow time for the transition to take place. Avoid making hasty judgments about your new life as a parent. Recognize the opportunities for change and new beginnings as your priorities and lifestyle are altered. Create new definitions for success. Refute the negative stereotypes often associated with the role of stay-at-home parent and be proud of your work as an at-home parent.

Join or start a parent's support group or playgroup to help you overcome feelings of isolation and get to know some new friends. Read supportive books and publications. Take advantage of your increased leisure time by starting a new hobby, broadening your skills and knowledge, spending more time by yourself, and nurturing your relationship with your partner. Realize that there are trade-offs to your work and family decisions, so make your decisions based on your personal and family priorities. Enjoy the little things and fleeting moments that make up part of your days, like watching your children develop, observing how they interact with a friend, or helping them complete their homework in a less rushed atmosphere.

Related Activity: As you begin adapting to the new rhythm of being an at-home parent, start setting daily, weekly and monthly goals for yourself. Be sure your goals are realistic and appropriate for your new situation. Break your projects into bite-size pieces that can be completed in concentrated blocks of time that are available to you when your baby is napping or when your children are at school.

Recommended Resources

1. *Home By Choice: Raising Emotionally Secure Children In An Insecure World* by Brenda Hunter (Multnomah Publishers Inc., 2000)
2. *Sequencing* by Arlene Rosen Cardozo (Brownstone Books, 1996)
3. *Staying Home: From Full-Time Professional To Full-Time Parent* by Darcie Sanders and Martha M. Bullen (Spencer & Waters, 1999)
4. *What's A Smart Woman Like You Doing At Home?* by Linda Burton, Janet Dittmer and Cheri Loveless, founders of the Mothers at Home Organization (Family & Home Network, 1992)
5. *Women Leaving The Workplace: How To Make The Transition From Work To Home* by Larry Burkett (Moody Press, 1999)

Mentor Your Children!

Children

> *Choose your battles wisely – you can win the battle but lose the war.*
> *~ Author Unknown*

TIP # 31 - ALLEVIATE THE POWER STRUGGLES

The power struggles you (may) face with your young children are often the #1 stress-causing issue for parents. According to Tim Jordan, MD, a behavioral pediatrician and author, the three main problem spots for most working parents with young children are:

1. **Morning routines**. Getting kids up, dressed, fed, and out the door on time each day (see Tip #33).
2. **Reuniting time**. Major fits and meltdowns when you reunite with your kids at the end of the day.
3. **Bedtime battles.** Bedtime battles that can go on for hours (see Tip #34).

The energy that working parents expend on worrying about whether or not they're doing a good job in their multiple roles of parent, spouse, employee/manager, or boss is often surpassed by the issues of power struggles with their children.

The first component you have to understand about the problem and its solution is the influence of your child's temperament on the power struggles. Children with inherent personality traits that cause them to be very intense, those with low adaptability to change and transition, those with a low frustration tolerance, and those with a low threshold for handling stimulation (e.g., noise, lights, and people) generally are more prone to power struggles.

It's also important to understand the influence of your child's developmental/behavioral stage. Young children between the ages of 18 months and four years are pushing limits, teasing, manipulating, and trying to engage adults in power struggles as part of their natural developmental phase. They experiment and learn from the reactions they receive. They learn boundaries and limits, how to handle their aggressions, and how to get along with others as they go through this phase.

Your reactions, and how you respond to the negative behaviors, will either worsen the undesired behaviors or redirect/prevent them. You'll want to manage your child's behavior without getting sucked into the struggle. If you frequently nag, remind, threaten, yell, spank, or give in, you are, unfortunately, contributing to a negative pattern of behaviors which results in more frequent, intense, and longer battles.

Here are some solutions to help you avoid, or at least alleviate, power struggles with your children:

- Detach yourself emotionally while your child's emotions spiral up and down. Stay as cool and calm as you can amidst the fury.
- Don't take things personally. Use your understanding of temperaments and developmental stages to disengage from the behavior and the emotional triggers.
- Use immediate kind and firm follow-through and a no-nonsense approach. Don't provide repeated warnings and idle threats. Instead, correct the undesirable behavior or action immediately.
- When your child is around three-years-old, he may be old enough to understand and participate in a discussion with you regarding behaviors and consequences. It's best to create agreements and consequences ahead of time rather than in the heat of the moment. Discuss and provide examples of both acceptable and unacceptable behavior. Spell out consequences that both you and your child can live with. Don't set a punishment you won't follow through on (e.g., no TV for the rest of your life!).
- Stick to routines and schedules as much as possible. Children respond better when they know what to expect. Establish routines particularly for your most troublesome times of day.

If you can reduce the number of power struggles in your home, your family life will become more peaceful, calm, and cooperative. Wouldn't you rather start and end your day peacefully?

Related Activity: Work to end the power struggles with your children. Talk to other parents and find out how they handle power struggles with their children and observe interactions between other parents and their children.

Recommended Resources

1. *Closing the Gap: A Strategy For Bringing Parents And Teens Together* by Jay McGraw (Simon & Schuster, 2001)
2. *Food Fights And Bedtime Battles: A Parent's Guide To Negotiating Daily Power Struggles* by Tim J. Jordan, MD (Berkley Publishing Group, 2001)
3. *Keeping Your Kids Grounded When You're Flying By The Seat Of Your Pants* by Tim Jordan, MD (Palmerston & Reed Publishing Company, 1999)
4. *Parenting Teens With Love And Logic: Preparing Adolescents For Responsible Adulthood* by Foster W. Cline and Jim Fay (Pinon Press, 1992)
5. *The 7 Habits Of Highly Effective Teens: The Ultimate Teenage Success Guide* by Stephen Covey (Simon & Schuster, 1998)
6. *Unplugging Power Struggles: Resolving Emotional Battles With Your Kids, Ages 2 To 10* by Jan Faull (Parenting Press, Inc., 1999)

> *Success is neither magical or mysterious. Success is the natural consequence of consistently applying the basic fundamentals.*
>
> ~ *Jim Rohn*

TIP # 32 - STAND BY YOUR RULES

In an attempt to achieve special time with their children, some working parents may be tempted to let discipline slide. After being apart for a good portion of the day, it's perfectly natural to want peaceful and happy family time. However, every family has to set limits and maintain certain values and systems in order to function effectively. Children, especially young ones, do better when routines are consistent and they know what to expect. Resist the urge to take what seems like the easy way out around discipline because it really is only a short-term solution.

There are lots of effective methods for maintaining discipline. Select something that works for you and use it consistently. Start while your children are young so that your authority is established well before they enter school. By knowing and understanding limits and rules, your children will also be better able to cope and adapt to school requirements and socialization.

Related Activity: Together with your partner, identify the behaviors and negative attitudes that your child possesses that need correction. Then prepare a list of 1–10 rules that are a priority for each child. (Older children may have more on their list of rules/priorities.) Spell out and illustrate precisely what's expected (and give an example for younger children). Determine privileges that your child enjoys that he has come to take for granted and that can be lost as a consequence of breaking the rules. Select about five privileges that really make a difference to your child. Encourage your children to follow the rules and let them know that when they don't, they will lose these privileges (in order) from the list. Remember to be calm when explaining the rules, but be consistent and patient while you work with your partner to enforce what you have communicated.

Recommended Resources

1. *1–2–3 Magic* by Thomas W. Phelan (Child Management, 1996)
2. *Positive Discipline A–Z: From Toddlers To Teens* by Jane Nelson (Prima Communications, Inc., 1999)
3. *Smart Discipline Program* by Larry Koenig & Associates. See www.smartdiscipline.com for more information, or call 1-800-255-3008
4. *The Discipline Book: How To Have A Better-Behaved Child From Birth To Age Ten* by William and Martha Sears (Brown & Company 1995)

> *We were made for calm, not chaos, and that is why we long for simpler times. Somewhere deep inside we know that simpler times are better times.*
>
> ~ *Thomas Kinkade*

TIP # 33 - AVOID THE MORNING MAYHEM

Mornings are an often a crazy time in many households because everyone is rushing around to get ready and out the door on time. Unfortunately, this frantic pace sets the tone for the rest of the day. When your morning activities run smoothly and you're out the door with ample time, it can make a significant difference in the rest of the day.

Employ a number of tactics to replace the high-anxiety-inducing, frenetic pace that exists now. Here are a few of my absolute favorite tactics to help you have a more peaceful morning routine:

- Prepare the night before.
- Awaken slightly earlier.
- Simplify the morning routines (and clothing choices).
- Enlist everyone's cooperation.
- Let go of perfection.
- Put on your watch first (or sleep with your watch on).
- Keep your household well-organized.
- Make it a game.
- Have a ready assortment of convenient breakfast foods.
- Get adequate sleep.

Related Activity: Start your bedtime rituals and routines about a half hour earlier tonight. Be firm about bedtime for your kids (and yourself!). Ensure that all clothes are laid out, special toys selected, homework done and packed up, and briefcases and book bags are at the door. The reward for this extra effort of planning and organizing will be a calmer morning, with more time spent together before hurrying off.

> *Break the tensions of daily living, or the tensions will break you.*
> ~ *Anonymous*

TIP # 34 - END SLEEPING BATTLES

For working parents, it is essential that you get a good night's sleep in order to effectively function the next day. A good night's sleep is important for the physical and emotional health of both you *and* your children. Unfortunately, more than 30% of today's parents continue to struggle with getting their children to go to bed by themselves and sleep through the night in their own bed. This problem is not unique to those with infants. Many older children awaken with nightmares and other sleep problems, as well. Some of the problems are caused by medical conditions such as middle ear infections, colic, teething, allergies and skin problems, while others are a result of patterns created by developed habits.

Although parents often believe it is important to help their children get to sleep, it is actually more important that your children learn how to fall asleep on their own. From their infancy, your children need to learn how to soothe themselves back to sleep if they wake up during the night. Too often parents will do anything that works (for better or worse) so that they can get back to sleep. It is important to know that good sleep habits are learned behaviors and infants with sleep problems usually grow up to be children with sleep problems.

Help your baby associate nighttime with darkness and sleep time by ensuring there is adequate darkness in the room. Let your baby nap during the day in the light and during the evening in a dark room. Do not let naps exceed three successive hours during the day so that your baby learns to associate long periods of sleep with nighttime. Although it may be difficult at first (especially for you!), place your baby in his crib awake without rocking, holding or feeding him until he falls off to sleep. Provide your baby with a favorite blanket or stuffed toy (make sure it meets safety requirements) to help ease the transition and help him feel secure. If he wakes up during the night, avoid stimulation, entertainment, or lights. Feed him, change the diaper, and then set him back down for sleep. It's also important to establish regular daily routines as soon as possible.

For older children, bedtime begins with a regular routine, as well. Establish a familiar and pleasant routine you can use in the evening to peacefully transition to bedtime. Many toddlers and older children will prolong bedtime and manipulate their parents as much as they can. Although you are probably tired from a hard day at work, do not succumb to their stall tactics. Just go through your established routine and get them off to their own bed.

Individual needs will determine the amount of sleep your children need in order to function adequately the next day. The bedtime is established based on your child's sleep requirements and your own needs for some time without your children. Creating a ritual that takes about a half hour will help them unwind and transition from day to night. Some examples of bedtime rituals include taking a bath, changing into pajamas, brushing their teeth, reading a story, talking about their day, a kiss, a hug, and a tuck under the covers. Avoid rough-housing, tickling or other stimulation at bedtime. Also, eliminate scary movies and violent television shows because they can cause nightmares. Most of the bedtime routine should take place in your child's bedroom so when the ritual is over, you leave their bedroom instead of your child leaving a different room. Your bedtime rituals should never be cancelled as a punishment.

For those of you with poorly established routines, creating new patterns may take some patience and practice. A child who is used to stalling at night will not give in so easily and a full-blown temper tantrum may result. It is important to be firm but loving at this point. Some pediatrician's recommend closing the child's bedroom door and opening it once they quiet, all the while remaining calmly outside their door and repeating that you will open the door once they quiet down. Conversation, urging, or cajoling just gives attention that reinforces the undesirable behavior. Keep reinforcing your rules and continue returning your child to his bed.

Another difficulty many working parents tell me about is that their children wake up in the middle of the night and want to crawl into bed with them. This behavior will prevent your children from learning how to cope on their own at night and will infringe on your privacy. When your children come into your room during the night, return them to their own bed promptly. Let your children know that if they happen to wake up during the night and can't get back to sleep, you want them to stay in their own bedroom. Be firm and consistent!

If, however, their nighttime waking is caused by a nightmare, your frightened child needs physical contact, comfort, and reassurance. Following the occurrence, most children can tell you what their bad dream was about; reassure your child that it's just a dream, stay with her for just a few minutes to calm her down and help her feel safe. You can discuss the nightmare in the morning. If frequent nightmares occur, consider your child's activities that may be contributing to the problem.

Night terrors are another problem sometimes exhibited by children between the ages of three- and eight-years-old. Unlike nightmares, night terrors develop earlier in the night and usually begin one to four hours after falling asleep. You find your child sitting up in bed screaming and thrashing about but not entirely awake. Your child's heart will be racing and his eyes will be wide open, sometimes even talking to you but not responding to your questions.

During night terrors, your child is usually not even aware of your presence, and may even push you away, sobbing and flailing more if touched or disturbed. You should resist trying to comfort or hold your child during a night terror because you may awaken him and cause him to become more disoriented. Your child is inconsolable for sometimes up to 30 minutes during a night terror until finally relaxing and falling back to sleep on his own. Use caution to ensure your child cannot hurt himself during a night terror. Fortunately, your child will probably not recall the incident in the morning.

Don't let your children manipulate you at bedtime or in the middle of the night. If a medical condition seems to exist, consult your doctor or pediatrician. Although you are probably tired yourself, don't leave yourself more vulnerable to their tactics to get attention or special privileges from you by giving in. Help your children develop good sleep habits. Many sleep problems can be prevented if you allow your children to fall asleep on their own and to go back to sleep on their own during periods of normal night waking.

Children must have periods of uninterrupted sleep in order to have optimal growth and development. And, besides that, a good night's sleep helps *you* perform better at your job and exhibit higher amounts of patience. (Good night!)

Related Activity: Establish a new bedtime routine to get your kids off to bed at the designated time. Reward your children with positive feedback each evening when they cooperate and praise them each morning that they wake up in their own bed.

Recommended Resources
1. *Healthy Sleep Habits, Happy Child* by Marc Weissbluth (Fawcett Books, 1999)
2. *Nighttime Parenting: How To Get Your Baby And Child To Sleep (La Leche League International Book)* by William Sears, MD and Mary White (Plume, 1999)
3. *The No-Cry Solution: Gentle Ways To Help Your Baby Sleep Through The Night* by Elizabeth Pantley and William Sears, MD (McGraw Hill/Contemporary Books, 2002)
4. *Solve Your Child's Sleep Problems* by Richard Ferber (Fireside, 1986)

> *Your children get a lot of good stuff out of your work. They benefit from the tales you tell over dinner. They learn from the things you explain to them about what you do. They brag about you at school. They learn that work is interesting, that it has a dignity, that it is necessary and pleasing, and that it is a perfectly natural thing for both mothers and fathers to do...Your work enriches your children more than it deprives them.*
>
> *~ Louise Lague*

TIP # 35 - HELP YOUR KIDS "GET" YOUR WORK

Children respect and accept your work better when they understand what you do and why. You can help your children understand your work by talking about it and, if possible, occasionally taking them there to see where you work. Tell your kids about at least one interesting thing that happened, something that you learned, or something that made you laugh each day. Helping your kids understand more about your work will also help them learn many important lessons about the world of work in general and help them feel more grown-up.

Concentrate on sharing the positive things about work more than the complaints about your boss, a difficult co-worker, trouble with a customer, or other stresses you might experience during your workday. Take photos of your workplace and of the people you work with and bring them home to stimulate a conversation about your work.

For those who work at home, invite your kids into your office for a quick tour, but keep your boundaries about your workspace. Help them understand the type of work you do, your customers/clients, your product/service, and the benefits you provide.

Related Activity: Make your work simple enough to understand so that your children can explain what you do for a living (and how it benefits others). (In fact, I was shocked when at a meeting with a new doctor my five-year-old answered the doctor's question about what we do for a living with, "my mom helps people make a better life and my dad is in charge of all the computers at work.")

Recommended Resources

1. *Ask The Children: The Breakthrough Study That Reveals How To Succeed At Work And Parenting* by Ellen Galinsky of the Families and Work Institute (Quill Publishing, 2000)
2. *Big Purple Mommy: Nurturing Our Creative Work, Our Children, And Ourselves* by Colleen Hubbard (Perigee, 2001)
3. *Daddy@Work* by Robert Wolgemuth (Zondervan, 2002)
4. *Mommy Works, Daddy Works* by Marika Pedersen and Midele Hall (Annick Press, 2000)
5. *My Mommy Works* by Roberta Chad (Achievers Technology Resource, Inc., 2001)
6. *Working: People Talk About What They Do All Day And How They Feel About What They Do* by Studs Terkel (New Press, 1997)

Nurture Your Children!

Family Time

> *We may miss a great deal of joy because we expect it to be unusual, dramatic, and spectacular. We are waiting for lights to flash and bells to ring. But the truth is that joy is here, right now, waiting for us to notice it.*
>
> ~ *Veronica Ray*

TIP # 36 - HAVE DINNER TOGETHER AS A FAMILY

Mealtime is an opportunity to have high-quality time together as a family. It should be a pleasant time for your family to relax and enjoy each other's company. Some simple strategies can make dinner time less hectic. Here are some tips you can implement:

- Establish a rule of no TV at dinner. (TV at any meal is a distraction and prevents communication from occurring; turn the TV off and talk to each other about your day instead.)
- Avoid arguing or fighting at the dinner table.
- Serve kids early. (If one spouse traditionally arrives home later than the other, prepare dinner for your kids as early as possible, then invite them to sit with you and your spouse while you have dinner and they have dessert.)
- Plan ahead. (Plan your menu for the week prior to going grocery shopping.)
- Marinade. (Before work, season and marinade that night's dinner, then refrigerate.)
- Have alternatives on-hand. (Serve a well-balanced dinner that gives everyone choices—insist that kids try a small portion of any new food and have regular favorites available.)
- Stir Fry. (Cut vegetables the night before, prior to leaving for work, or buy a pre-cut frozen mixed blend and slice meats while still slightly frozen, then store it all in the refrigerator until ready to use later.)
- Grill, Sauté and Broil. (Select foods that require little cooking time such as steaks, chops, fish and boneless chicken breasts.)

- Pack your freezer. (Prepare larger portions than you'll need for your meal and freeze half so you can quickly thaw and heat a home-cooked meal.)
- Stock the basics. (Keep an assortment of ingredients on-hand in your cupboards and be inventive and creative with ways to prepare or present your meals.)

Related Activity: Follow the tips above to have a family dinner two nights this week. Gradually work up to having dinner together 5–7 nights per week. Make dinner a pleasant time for your family to relax together and enjoy each other's company. If dinner together is absolutely impossible, plan ahead each day and make breakfast or lunch your special meal.

Recommended Resources

1. *Quick Meals For Healthy Kids And Busy Parents: Wholesome Family Recipes In 30 Minutes Or Less* by Sandra K. Nissenberg, Margaret L. Bogle, and Audrey C. Wright (John Wiley & Sons, Inc., 1995)
2. *The Once-A-Week Cooking Plan: The Incredible Cooking Program That Will Save You 10-20 Hours A Week (And Have Your Family Begging For More)* by Joni Hilton (Prima Communications, Inc., 1999)
3. *The Organized Parent: 365 Simple Solutions To Managing Your Home, Your Time, And Your Family's Life* by Christina Baglivi Tinglov (McGraw-Hill/Contemporary, 2002)
4. *The Working Family's Cookbook* by Irena Chalmers (Barron's Educational Series, Inc., 1993)

> At the end of life, it's the laughter, the tears, the shared joys and the shared heartaches we remember. The wealth, the work, the trials, and problems are as nothing. It's the quality of our days and the people we share them with that makes the difference.
>
> ~ Margaret James

TIP # 37 - CREATE WEEKEND RITUALS

Shared weekend rituals are especially important for families with working parents. By spending enjoyable time together you create happy memories for today and tomorrow. Planning your activities (e.g., doing chores; visiting Grandma; going to the movies, church/synagogue, shopping, miniature golfing, kite flying, or walking on the beach) helps both parents and children feel more involved with each other. Doing the household chores helps create a feeling of shared responsibility for getting the work of the family done. A child who actively participates in both the fun and the work of their family is bound to feel more valued and grown-up.

Rituals are actions we take thoughtfully and purposefully to celebrate and even transform our relationships with the people we care about. The better we understand rituals, the more their power will enrich our lives.

Related Activity: Decide on a special tradition you can start this weekend such as pancakes on Sunday morning, Friday night pizza and games, a visit to someone special on Saturday afternoon. Enjoy each other's company!

Recommended Resources

1. *Putting Family First: Successful Strategies For Reclaiming Family Life In A Hurry Up World* by William J. Doherty, PhD (Carlson Owl Books, 2002)
2. *The Intentional Family: Simple Rituals To Strengthen Family Ties* by Willaim, J. Doherty (Avon Books 1999)
3. *The Over-Scheduled Child: Avoiding The Hyper-Parenting Trap* by Alvin Rosenfeld MD and Nicole Wise, (Griffin Trade Paperback, 2001)

> *You've got to decide on an inner discipline to protect yourself. Step out of the interesting dynamic rhythm every so often and focus on your internal life.*
>
> ~ *Naomi Rosenblatt*

TIP # 38 - INSTITUTE A DO NOTHING DAY ONCE A MONTH

Life is so incredibly busy. Step out of your fast-paced lifestyle and try "cocooning" (as described below) in order to slow down your life once in awhile. The change of pace of staying at home for an extended period of time will provide an opportunity for some mental downtime.

One day each month declare a "Do Nothing Day" to cocoon together. During this day, have no visitors or play dates, no agendas, no fix-it projects, no housework, no "fixing" meals, no phones—just do nothing. Create a totally simplistic day that you can use to reconnect as a family, hang out, play games, and pretty much do nothing (unless you are all compelled to do it together for fun). Stock up on some essential snacks and foods the day before your "Do Nothing Day." Inform your friends, neighbors, and family that you will not be accepting any visitors. You can live on "easy fixings" like sandwiches, carrot sticks and the like, or take-out food. Eat whenever you are hungry and follow the natural rhythms of each individual and the family as a whole.

At first you may get some resistance because many people become accustomed to the frantic over-scheduled pace of life. But, after holding this special day for a couple of months, it will probably become a well sought after respite and a fun family tradition. Your family (and you) will actually begin looking forward to a day free of distractions and noise from the outside world.

Related Activity: Do you live in your house or just enter and exit it on your way to somewhere else? Create a day within your own home that revolves around life's simplicities. How would your day be different or the same as the one described above? Do nothing, and enjoy the day together with your family.

> *Nothing valuable can be lost by taking time.*
>
> *~ Abraham Lincoln*

TIP # 39 - MAKE PLANS FOR NO PLANS

Replenishing yourself by doing nothing is important for your body, mind, and spirit. Create a time each day when you can relax, either through meditation, centering, or whatever you choose. Additionally, create time with your partner when you do nothing except go for a walk together, spend time talking, eating, or playing. With your kids, be in the moment and take advantage of the opportunities as they occur.

Don't fall into the trap of scheduling every minute of every day. Structure periods into your week where absolutely nothing is planned.

Related Activity: Leave a block of unscheduled time on your calendar this week. Take a morning, afternoon, evening, or better yet, a whole day and give yourself the opportunity for no appointments or obligations. Stop and ask yourself, "What do I really want to do right now?" and do whatever comes to mind in the moment. Trust your gut instincts and act now.

Recommended Resource

The Art Of Doing Nothing: Simple Ways To Make Time For Yourself by Veronique Vienne (Crown Publishing Group, 1998)

Avoid Over-Planning!

> *The key is not to prioritize what's on your schedule, but to schedule your priorities.*
>
> ~ *Stephen R. Covey*

TIP # 40 - MAXIMIZE YOUR TIME WITH CHERISHED ONES

Although you may perceive that you have less time and feel more rushed today, people actually have more leisure time and opportunities than in the past. To save time on the endless chores and tasks that must be accomplished and gain snippets of quality time, try out some of these ideas:

- **Share household responsibilities.** Have your kids and spouse share the responsibilities at home with you. Agree on which chores each person will be responsible for and hold him or her accountable. Use positive reinforcement rather than punishment to help get the desired results. Don't redo what they do—just keep teaching and reinforcing how you want it done. Accept the imperfect from your family because the more they do, the less there is for you to do (see Tip #41).
- **Consolidate shopping trips.** Plan ahead and consolidate your trips to the store to minimize your need to go shopping; going often is a big time waster. Utilize shopping services if you really prefer not to do this one.
- **Post a central calendar.** Use a calendar to post everyone's activities and commitments. This helps you avoid double-booking and alerts you of upcoming events. Use lists to help you remember what you have to do and post them by your calendar so that they don't get lost and can more easily be incorporated into your daily schedule.
- **Optimize travel time.** Converse with your kids while going to and from activities. They may respond better this way than in a face-to-face conversation. You can use this captive audience time to discuss important matters.
- **Set priorities.** Decide what's important to you and establish limits and boundaries to protect it (see Tips # 19, 20, 21).

- **Get homework done.** Set up a time and place for homework. Stock up on anticipated supplies and materials. Be sure you understand teacher's expectations. Often, parents push kids to do more than the teacher expects and ultimately end up with an unnecessary battle on their hands.
- **Use e-mail and messaging.** Avoid lengthy phone conversations by utilizing e-mail and instant messaging. Create and use lists so that you can quickly send the same message to a number of people. Save templates of your routine e-mails so that you don't have to continuously re-create them. Make important calls when your kids are occupied and less likely to interrupt.
- **Get a fresh start.** Begin each day after adequate rest and you'll have greater efficiency. Start each day with a warm greeting to your family and help get everyone's day off to a pleasant start. A pleasant start sets the foundation for the rest of the day. Avoid haggling over petty things. Choose your battles wisely and do not let tension fester.

Related Activity: Create the space and opportunity to have more quality time with your children by eliminating some of the activities in your life and/or theirs. Share the decision-making process so that you're working jointly at creating more time together rather than feeling like you're taking something away as a punishment.

Recommended Resources

1. *2003 Moms Family Wall Calendar* (Workman Publishing Company, Inc., 2002)

2. *The GO MOM!*™ *Planner (An ultimate catchall day planner for everything that is family)* by Molly Gold. Available exclusively at www.gomominc.com/

Success for Super Busy Parents

Key Essential #5

ENJOY LIFE

Stop the frenzy of working longer and enjoying life less. Create opportunities for fun, relaxation, and personal growth. Realign your life around what's most important to you. Live by your values and priorities.

Spouse/Significant Other

> *The greatest good we can do for others is not to share OUR riches, but to assist in revealing their OWN.*
>
> ~ *Benjamin Disraeli*

TIP # 41 - SHARE THE LOAD

Especially in a dual-career household, both parents need to learn to share the household responsibilities and childcare. Many households today still see the housework as the woman's job. Fact is, men don't usually volunteer to share half the workload for children or elders. However, the housework is the whole family's job. If it's important for Mom to work, it's just as important for everyone to share the chores.

Sharing halfway along the line may be too rigid, but there are ways to divide up family demands that can be acceptable to everyone. Planning meetings are a must! Sharing feelings about the workload and your expectations are even more important than sharing the work. Everyone needs to participate. If everyone in a family with working parents does their share, time together is increased and enriched.

When both you and your spouse work full-time, both of you can do one-and-a-half jobs, instead of leaving the wife with what amounts to two full-time jobs: a career and parenting. You can off-load some of the domestic duties by determining to pay for them or by paying for extra services such as pick-up, delivery, personal shoppers or chefs. Rather than accepting all the workload and eventually resenting your partner, talk about it and find a way to work it out. Think of it as a challenge you *must* solve.

Urge your legislators, employer, and your industry to offer better services to support the needs of working parents.

Related Activity: Make a list of all the chores that must be done on a daily, weekly, and monthly basis in your home. Include everything! Next, have a family meeting to decide how each chore will be accomplished, by whom, and how frequently. Be sure to involve everyone in the household starting with your three-year-old and up. Kids love to feel important by contributing and having their own responsibilities. Let everyone begin by selecting those chores they enjoy doing and divvy up whatever is remaining. Accept that some chores will not be completed to your standards (see Tip #12); don't nag to get them done. Allow everyone the chance to have responsibilities of their own. When everyone in the family shares in the workload the whole house will run more smoothly. Get your family on board!

Recommended Resources

1. *Chore Wars: How Households Can Share The Work And Keep The Peace* by James Thornton (Red Wheel/Weiser, 1997)
2. *Partnership Tools: Transforming The Way We Live Together* by Alan Konell (Hippo Press, 2001)

> *No one can make you feel inferior without your consent.*
> ~ *Eleanor Roosevelt*

TIP # 42 - BALANCE THE HOUSEHOLD CONTRIBUTIONS

In some families today, the wife is the primary breadwinner. Although this may conflict with your personal beliefs or societal pressures, it's important to make adjustments in the balance of power within your family.

In America, recent statistics by the US Bureau of Labor show that one in three working wives make more than her husband—up from one in five in 1980. There are varied reasons for the higher earnings of women today, including more education, different professional choices, expanded opportunities, and layoffs of the husband who might previously have been the breadwinner. Women are using more of their potential than in past years, and more of a woman's identity and personal fulfillment come from her career now, too.

The shame often felt by men who lose their "breadwinner" status is not only unnecessary but also very self-destructive. Regardless of which spouse earns more money, it is more important that in two-parent families, both spouses contribute meaningfully to the household. Identify your own roles and responsibilities that support and respect the partnership and each other.

Here are some tips to help minimize conflict:

- Avoid continuously bringing up the fact that you're the higher wage earner as a way of stating your power.
- Communicate your feelings honestly if you feel you're being treated unfairly or if you think you're being controlled by the higher wage earner. (Be open to your partner's feelings and encourage their communication.)
- Treat your marriage as a partnership in which both of you can benefit from having more money coming into the household, regardless of who's earning it.

- Create new models of marriage that work for your unique situation if the old models (and role definitions) are causing conflict.

Related Activity: If you and your spouse experience any conflict or tension regarding the wage earning ratios in your household, talk about your feelings and re-negotiate ways to handle the household money and decision-making so both of you feel comfortable, valued, and respected.

Recommended Resources

1. *Marital Equality: Its Relationship To The Well-Being Of Husbands And Wives* by Janice M. Steil (Sage Publications, 1997)
2. *The New Couple: Why The Old Rules Don't Work And What Does,* by Maurice Taylor and Seana McGee (Harper Collins, 2000)
3. *Two Careers/One Family: The Promise Of Gender Equality* by Lucia Albino Gilbert (Sage Publications, 1993)
4. *Who Supports the Family?: Gender And Breadwinning In Dual-Earner Marriages* by Jean L. Potuchek (Stanford University Press, 1997

Respect Your Spouse's Contributions!

> *Whoever said love is blind is dead wrong. Love is the only thing that lets us see each other.*
>
> *~ Martha Beck*

TIP # 43 - TAKE CARE OF YOUR MARRIAGE

Children and work take much of your time, attention, and energy and can strain even the best of marriages. Your attention is diverted in a dozen ways and your spouse is often far from the top of the list. Although your spouse is an adult who can take care of themselves and attend to their needs, there is a give-and-take motion in a loving human relationship, and it needs your attention.

Find a way to reconnect with your spouse as partners. Re-commit to the vows you once shared to love, honor, and cherish each other until death do you part. Take a break from the kids to spend some time together. Discuss things that bother you and things that you dream of. Talk about things that are going on in the world, politics, the news, sports, places to go, people to visit, and the qualities that attracted you to each other.

Related Activity: Leap over all the obstacles and responsibilities this week and make time for you and your spouse a priority. Arrange a date, and, if necessary, invite another couple to join you and help out the conversation. Do your best to avoid touchy discussions about your kids, work, or home projects. Use some imagination and find a special way to start connecting on a more meaningful level. Get to know each other all over again!

Recommended Resources

1. *Getting The Love You Want: A Guide For Couples* by Harville Hendricks, PhD (Owl Books, 2001)
2. *The Seven Principles For Making Marriage Work* by John Mordechai Gottman and Nan Silver (Three Rivers Press, 2000)
3. *Why Marriages Succeed Or Fail...And How You Can Make Yours Last* by John Mordechai Gottman, Nan Silver (Contributor) (Fireside, 1995)

> *There is no greater feeling than being loved and nothing that makes our spirit soar more than the feeling that we are worthy of love!*
> ~ *Michael Nottelman*

TIP # 44 - REKINDLE ROMANCE

Your relationship with your partner is the cornerstone of your family's stability and happiness. Yet you often get so immersed in outside responsibilities that you neglect putting focused time and energy into that relationship. With hectic work schedules and multiple demands from your kids and other sources it may often seem like there's no time for romance.

For parents, romance in the parenting sector, may need to be planned rather than to expect spontaneous happenings. Either planned or spontaneous, here are some simple romantic ideas that you can do for little or no money:

- Be kids again...have fun at the playground, skating, sledding, or visiting the aquarium or zoo.
- Cook a meal together.
- Cuddle up on a hayride, horse-and-buggy or sleigh ride.
- Enjoy an outdoor concert.
- Give a passionate, affectionate kiss.
- Give a warm embracing hug.
- Go for a walk hand-in-hand.
- Go to a movie matinee or watch a movie at home.
- Go to your local community theatre or "plays in the park."
- Kiss hello, kiss goodbye.
- Make focused time for each other.
- Make love.
- Meet for lunch.
- Picnic on your living room floor.
- Spend a day at the beach.
- Take a bubble bath or shower together.
- Take a class together (dance, gourmet cooking, massage, travel, money, etc.).

- Talk to each other...share feelings and communicate regularly!
- Tour a museum.
- Tune in and really listen.
- Write a love note or send a greeting card.

You'll undoubtedly have more physical and emotional energy, as well as love to give your children if you are satisfied as a couple. Sometimes it's easy to lose sight of what's important in life. When holidays (like Valentines Day) come it's easy to get wrapped up in the obligatory pomp and circumstance of the tradition and tend to forget the simpler, more important reasons why you celebrate. Hopefully, you do some of this already, but a little extra fuss once in a while goes a long way!

Related Activity: Do something romantic with your partner. Don't wait for your partner to take the lead. Plan an activity or be creative and spontaneous today!

Recommended Resources

1. *Love Life For Parents* by David Arp and Claudia Arp (Zondervan Publishing House, 1998)
2. *Rekindle The Passion While Raising Your Kids* by Anthony J. Garascia (Sorin Books, 2001)
3. *Romantic At-Home Dinners: Sneaky Strategies For Couples With Kids* by Nan Booth and Gary Fischler (Brighton Publications, 1994)

> *Love is not finding the perfect person, but finding the imperfect person perfect.*
>
> *~ Unknown*

TIP # 45 - ACKNOWLEDGE YOUR MATE

It's very easy to ignore your own needs between the daily stresses of work and home, and it's even easier to inadvertently ignore your mate in the process. You must maintain a healthy relationship with your mate. Let your mate know how much you appreciate having them in your life. As you organize your children's activities and your work life, be sure to also organize time for yourself and opportunities for you as a couple (see Tip #44 for romantic ideas). This will help your family run well and increase everyone's happiness levels.

Although sometimes you may feel angry with your mate for not doing their share of the burden at home, start acknowledging the contributions he does make. Shift your attitude from "he doesn't do enough" to "I'm so grateful he does _____." Communicate specifically what you need from your partner. Don't expect him to be a mind reader and just know what you need.

With my husband's work schedule and long commute, we can go days without really seeing each other. To compensate, we frequently call each other during the day to share important information or just to say, "I love you." Sometimes we send e-mail messages or the free greetings cards found on the Internet just to perk up the other with a warm virtual hug. I've let go of berating him for the little things that he doesn't do and have learned the importance of focusing on expressing my appreciation for what he *does* do. This has produced more respect, love, and kindness in our relationship and in our home.

Related Activity: Surprise your mate today with an e-mail greeting card or leave a card tucked in his briefcase, under the pillow, or any place it will likely be found during the day. Express at least one thing that you are grateful for in your relationship.

Recommended Resources

1. *A Couple's Guide To Communication* by John Mordechai Gottman (Research Press, 1979)
2. *Fighting For Your Marriage: Positive Steps For Preventing Divorce And Preserving A Lasting Love* by Howard J. J. Markman (John Wiley & Sons, Inc., 2001)
3. *Men Are From Mars, Women Are From Venus: A Practical Guide For Improving Communication And Getting What You Want In Your Relationships* by John Gray (Harper Collins Publishers, 1992)
4. *Ten Stupid Things Couples Do To Mess Up Their Relationships* by Laura C. Schlessinger (Harper Collins Publishers, 2001)

Revive Your Romance!

Friends and Extended Family

> *The most important single ingredient in the formula of success is knowing how to get along with people.*
>
> *~ Theodore Roosevelt*

TIP # 46 - BUILD A SUPPORT NETWORK

Having a number of trusted people and resources available just in case you need them in an unforeseen emergency (or even on a daily basis) will give you incredible peace of mind. Create a network of friends, relatives, neighbors, bosses, work colleagues, and various professionals to be a part of your support team. You can turn to them for advice, consultation, or outside information in order to assure you the opportunity to do your best as a parent and as a productive worker.

Have an array of friends and family members you can turn to to talk out issues that arise with your children. Choose friends you admire for their experience, insight, or interest in helping you. Enlist the support of those whose lives reflect the values and beliefs you admire and respect. Use the wealth of wisdom, experience, and perspective from those of an older generation who have already successfully raised their own children. Also use professional advisors capable of addressing specific concerns or problems such as pediatricians, family counselors, teachers, or learning specialists.

At work, gain support from people with skills unlike your own. There are people with complimentary skills and those with skills that completely differ. It's always helpful to know some technical people, financial experts, and human resources professionals to assist you or guide you to quick solutions to problems you face. Identify people who can be part of your "success team." Build relationships with others and help them gain confidence in your abilities by your performance and results.

Ask specifically for what you need. Learn who is home during the day in your neighborhood. Get your children involved, too—work together as a team. Create back-up and emergency plans; always have a contingency. You must be willing to ask for help and allow yourself to receive it.

Related Activity: Ask two new people to be a part of your support network. (Example: In creating a list of people to contact in case of emergency, call a neighbor and ask them if they would be a contact for your child's school just in case you are temporarily unreachable. Make a point of getting to know this person a little better so that you are comfortable with them as a back-up.) Be clear in communicating how you want them to help you now or in the future. Begin establishing the relationships now.

Recommended Resources

1. *Creating Community Anywhere: Finding Support And Connection In A Fragmented World* by Carolyn R. Shaffe and Kristin Anundsen (Perigee, 1993)
2. *Stay-at-Home Parent Survival Guide: Real-Life Advice From Moms, Dads, And Other Experts A To Z* by Christina Baglivi Tinglov (McGraw-Hill/Contemporary, 2000)
3. *The Woman Source Catalog & Review: Tools For Connecting The Community For Women* by Ilene Rosoff (Celestial Arts, 1997)

> *The only way to have a friend is to be one.*
>
> *~ Ralph Waldo Emerson*

TIP # 47 - BROADEN YOUR SOCIAL CIRCLE

Working parents often have a very small social circle. Too often, you feel guilty when you take "time away" from your family to be with your friends; time with your friends and peers contributes to your well-being and health. In fact, an extensive set of research studies has revealed that people who don't enjoy a strong social network of extended family and friends are 2–3 times more likely to die at a younger age than those who do; women who report close ties with friends view their lives as being less stressful and more enjoyable.

Overwhelmed by the demands on your time, energy, and emotions, it's easy to blow off your friends and rationalize that it's more important for you to spend your nonworking hours with your family. However, friendships are important and needn't fall to the bottom of the list every time! Weave friendships back into your life and give yourself permission to enjoy them.

No one needs to feel alone or isolated. Begin nurturing your old friendships and creating new ones. A long lost friend will undoubtedly be surprised but will probably welcome your call (e-mail, card or letter) and look forward to getting together. Reconnect and maintain ties with former colleagues, classmates, and neighbors, too. You can talk about memories and laugh about the past as you get to know each other once again.

Generally, there are plenty of opportunities to meet new people through playgroups, support groups, reading groups, the gym, religious affiliations, and within your local neighborhood. Leagues, teams, and clubs exist for bowlers, golfers, tennis players, and almost any other hobby or interest you might have. If you are a member of a co-op, get to know other group members while you are volunteering your time. (Note: co-ops exist in many areas for childcare, nursery school, gardening, and shopping services.)

You can create new friendships at work, too. Although work friendships are often complicated, it's worthwhile to forge ahead and create a few relationships with people you can confide in, go out to lunch with, go for a walk with, carpool, or mentor. You may even be able to start a network or group within your work location. (One of my clients started a working mothers group within her sales office that later grew to include the entire corporation.) Once a community is created and the word is out, people with similar interests will come.

The Internet also has many groups and communities that may appeal to you. You can find them by using a keyword search in your search engine (e.g., "working moms," "stay at home parents," "single parents," "work at home," "dads as primary caregivers"). You can go on-line and visit chat rooms to talk with others who share your interests or challenges. (For your own safety and security, make it a practice never to meet new people in private places or give out personal information until you have established some rapport and trust. Use your best judgment!)

There are many organizations to choose from to help build your social and business network. Professional associations exist for nearly every trade. Organizations like the Rotary Club, Kiwanis, NAFE (National Association for Female Executives), and the NAWBO (National Association of Women Business Owners) often have local or virtual chapters.

For those who are not interested in large groups, you can get to know people within the group one-on-one or create friendships through other sources. Think outside the box! Decide what type of people you'd like to spend your time with...Where are they? Who are they? What do they spend their free time doing? When can you find them? What would they like about spending time with you? Make your intentions clear and see who you attract. Don't forget the parents of your childrens' friends—you already have numerous things in common related to your children!

Related Activity: Take a step toward making a new friend this week. Invite someone for coffee, offer to pick up another parent's child from the ball game, talk to the person working out next to you on the treadmill, meet a colleague for lunch, go for a drink with the gang after work, or get to know your child's friends' parents by giving them a call. Remember, other working parents are probably just as busy and (possibly) lonely as you are. Reach out and enjoy your new acquaintances and nurture your friendships.

Recommended Resources

1. *Friendshifts: The Power Of Friendship And How It Shapes Our Lives* by Jan Yager (Hannacroix Creek Books, Inc., 1999)
2. *How To Start A Conversation And Make Friends* by Don Gabor (Simon & Schuster Trade Publications, 2000)
3. *How To Win Friends & Influence People* by Dale Carnegie (Simon & Schuster, 1982)

> *The best index to a person's character is (a) how he treats people who can't do him any good, and (b) how he treats people who can't fight back.*
>
> *~ Abigail Van Buren*

TIP # 48 - EMBRACE DIVERSITY

Beyond more obvious racial, sexual, religious, and physical differences there are so many personality and behavioral styles in the people you know and interact with. Your children may at times seem like they're somebody else's because their temperament, traits, talents, and abilities may be so different from your own. Additionally, the people you work with will have many differences in the way they think, act, and approach work. I invite you to consider that none of this behavior is right or wrong...just different than your own, thus removing judgment from the equation.

People are different. We all have our own worthy contributions to make. You can honor the diversity by understanding it, respecting it, appreciating it, and finding ways to bring out other people's natural gifts and strengths.

It's the differences in people that create and balance a group, a team of people, or a family.

Related Activity: Recognize the differences in all of the people you know and focus on the strengths and qualities you like best. Rather than trying to change them to be the way you want them to be, change *you* to accept them the way they are.

Use a personality or behavior assessment type tool (e.g., Myers-Briggs Type Indicator or DISC Personal Profile) to gain a better understanding of your natural styles and how you relate to others. When groups or teams assess and understand their differences they can grow and accomplish more because of better communication and utilization of each individual's strengths.

There are only four kinds of people in this world: Those who have been caregivers, those who currently are caregivers, those who will be caregivers, and those who need caregivers.

~ Jack A. Nottingham

TIP # 49 - SEEK GUIDANCE WHEN CARING FOR AN ELDERLY PARENT

Many adult children assist their parents and relatives with their personal and medical care needs. If you are one of these adult children, sandwiched between your work, family, and your parent you know how the stress can mount when you combine your caregiving responsibilities with your family, personal obligations, and your career.

As a caregiver, you may experience depleted financial resources due to medical expenses not covered by insurance. You may also endure problems at work due to your high-rate of absenteeism and loss of productivity. Marital and family problems are not uncommon due to the pull for your time and attention.

Many caregivers rely on their instincts, common sense, and past experiences when assuming care giving responsibilities. But, it usually doesn't take long before the caregiver needs to seek help. Most turn to other family members, relatives, friends, and doctors for advice and support.

In addition, there are also numerous agencies and programs serving the elderly that are available to assist caregivers with their responsibilities. These resources include county, state, and national agencies that help caregivers. There are also magazines, newsletters, videos, books, training courses, support groups, and Web sites that offer varied advice and assistance.

Related Activity: If you anticipate that you will need to assume care-giving responsibilities, prepare yourself before the crisis moment occurs. Check in your area to find what programs are available to support you. Speak with others in this role to see how they manage.

Recommended Resources

1. *Boomer Basics: Everything That You Need To Know About The Issues Facing You, Your Children And Your Parents* by Robert Abrams and Walter T. Burke (McGraw-Hill Trade, 2000)
2. *Caring For Your Aging Parents: When Love Is Not Enough* by Barbara Deane (Deane Word Publishing, 1989)
3. *Caring For Yourself While Caring For Your Aging Parents: How To Help, How To Survive* by Claire Berman (Owl Books, 2001)
4. *The Fearless Caregiver: How To Get The Best Care For Your Loved One And Still Have A Life of Your Own* by Gary Barg (Editor) (Capital Books Inc., 2001)
5. *The Resourceful Caregiver: Helping Family Caregivers Help Themselves* by National Family Caregivers Association Staff (Mosby-Year Book, 1996)
6. *Two Jobs, No Life: Learning To Balance Work And Home* by Peter Marshall (Key Porter Books, 2002)

Success for Super Busy Parents

Key Essential #6

BUILD A SUPPORT NETWORK THAT WORKS FOR YOU.

Gain support from a variety of resources, people, and organizations. Nurture the relationships that matter most. Discover innovative ways to contribute to others, as well.

Part 3

BALANCE YOUR WORK LIFE

Work/Life Balance

> *Now and then it's good to pause in our pursuit of happiness and just be happy.*
>
> ~ *Guillaume Apollinaire*

TIP # 50 - PROGRESS TO A FULLY INTEGRATED AND BALANCED LIFE

Balance is essential to maintaining quality in life and work. It is a factor in taking good care of yourself and serving others. The quick assessment on the next two pages will help you determine where you have a good balance in your life and where you can use some adjustments to have more of an integrated and balanced life.

Related Activity: Complete the self-assessment to measure the degree of balance you have between the demands of work, family responsibilities, and personal time. Be extremely honest with yourself and see what this evaluation reveals for you.

Recommended Resources

1. *Balancing Act: How Managers Can Integrate Successful Careers And Fulfilling Personal Lives (Jossey-Bass Management Series)* by Joan Kofodimos (Jossey-Bass, 1993)
2. *Home And Work: Negotiating Boundaries Through Everyday Life* by Christena E. Nippert-Eng (University of Chicago Press, 1996)
3. *Lifebalance: Balancing Work With Family And Personal Needs: Balancing Structure With Spontaneity, Balancing Achievements With Relationships* by Linda Eyre and Richard Eyre (Fireside, 1997)
4. *Work And Family: Essays From The Work And Family Column Of The Wall Street Journal* by Sue Shellenbarger (Random House, Inc., 1999)

Work/Life Balance Assessment

	(Never----------Always)					
	0	1	2	3	4	5
SELF						
I have enough time for me (physically, mentally, emotionally, and spiritually).						
I take good care of myself.						
I effectively manage my finances.						
I live by my values and priorities.						
I have strong boundaries to protect and strengthen myself.						
TOTAL						
FAMILY						
I spend quality time with each person in my family.						
My children help with the household responsibilities.						
My children are healthy and adjusted.						
I resolve issues with my spouse regularly.						
I have a variety of people to support me and my family.						
TOTAL						
WORK						
My work is fulfilling and satisfying to me.						
My salary is commensurate with my skills and experience.						
I have opportunities to grow and advance myself personally and professionally.						
My work expends a healthy part of my life without overconsuming my personal or family time.						
I plan and organize my work to focus on the top priorities.						
TOTAL						

GRAND TOTAL: _____

Scoring: Overall high scores indicate more of an integrated and balanced life. A high score in only one area suggests an imbalance. If you have a high score in only one area you'll need to devote more time and energy to the other areas in order to create more integration in your life.

60-75	A well-balanced life. Keep up the good work!
45-59	A fair balance with some room for improvement. Consciously work on improving your life in an area where you feel out-of-balance.
30-44	You're barely integrating your home, career, and personal needs. Perhaps working with a professional coach can help you regain some balance in your life. Get some support!
Under 30	Create an action plan to integrate your life. Work with a professional counselor/therapist to resolve issues preventing you from having a better balance.

> *Be aware of wonder. Live a balanced life— learn some and think some and draw and paint and sing and dance and play and work every day some.*
>
> ~ *Robert (L.) Fulghum*

TIP # 51 - CONQUER THE CHALLENGES OF WORK AND FAMILY

As life continues to speed up and technology provides opportunities for you to do more, many people feel further away from living a balanced life. One of the central concerns of all working parents is to live a balanced life. But life is fluid and in constant motion, therefore the challenges you face are continually shifting and evolving. Find the formula that works for you and avoid the should's, could's, and have to's...they reflect someone else's standards rather than your own.

Learn to look, not for a solution, but for a *process*...a way of addressing your challenges that you can use over and over as each one arises. Just as you weigh the pros and cons of each course of action at work, set goals and objectives, organize your work, delegate, and communicate, you will be greatly helped if you learn to bring this level of concentration, focus, and discipline to your life at home. Interestingly, the same skills that contribute to your success at work and make you a valued productive employee are the skills that will help you manage your home life and achieve a healthy balance.

Some of the common challenges facing working parents today include: time for self, relationships, and family; being able to organize at home and work; sticking to priorities; professional development and career growth; societal standards; conflicting demands and sheer exhaustion. You can combat some of these challenges if you:

- Keep a healthy perspective.
- Rethink the 'should's, 'could's, 'have to', 'ought's, and 'if only's in your life.
- Acknowledge and accept your reality and current situation.
- Recognize your limitations.
- Have a positive attitude.

- Align your actions and how you handle everyday tasks and demands with what is *most* important to you (seek the *joy* in life and you'll end up feeling more balanced and happy).
- Commit to make changes to simplify your life and eliminate the habits that no longer serve you.

The stress of balancing work and family life can make you feel out of control. It can negatively affect your health and self-esteem. Feeling in control increases your ability to cope and feel better about yourself. The end result is that you will be a more productive worker and a more loving parent and partner.

Related Activity: Begin regaining control in your life by using the skills (you already have) that will help you achieve a healthy balance. Be aware of where your life is causing you the most stress and begin taking specific concrete actions to gain greater satisfaction and control. You can achieve a healthy balance in your life and successfully manage both work and family. It takes practice, but it's totally doable!

Recommended Resources

1. *Business Dad: How Good Businessmen Can Make Great Fathers (And Vice Versa)* by Tom Hirschfeld and Julie Hirschfeld (Little Brown & Company, 2000)
2. *Getting It Right: How Working Mothers Successfully Take Up The Challenge Of Life, Family And Career* by Laraine T. Zappert *(Pocket Books, 2002)*
3. *She Works/He Works: How Two-Income Families Are Happy, Healthy And Thriving* by Rosalind C. Barnett and Caryl Rivers (Harvard University Press, 1998)
4. *The Working Parents Help Book* by Susan Crites Price and Tom Price (Peterson's Press, 1994)
5. *Two Jobs, No Life: Learning To Balance Work And Home* by Peter Marshall (Key Porter Books, 2002)
6. *What's Happening To Home: Balancing Work, Life And Refuge In The Information Age* by Maggie Jackson (Sorin Books, 2002)

7. *Work and Family—Allies Or Enemies?: What Happens When Business Professionals Confront Life Choices* by Stewart D. Friedman and Jeffrey H. Greenhaus (Oxford University Press, 2000)

8. *Working Fathers: New Strategies For Balancing Work And Family* by James A. Levine and Todd L. Pittinsky (Perseus Publishing, 1997)

9. *Working Parents, Happy Kids: Strategies For Staying Connected* by Pati Crofut and Joanna Knapp (Turnagain Press, 1999)

Create an Integrated Life!

> *You must first be who you really are, then, do what you need to do, in order to have what you want.*
>
> *~ Margaret Young*

TIP # 52 - BALANCE COMPANY NEEDS WITH YOUR PERSONAL NEEDS

When you put your company's needs before your personal needs you put your life at risk. When your health, well-being, or relationships are neglected, you ultimately become less effective at work and in the rest of your life.

The key to balance is to become more productive and effective at work while enjoying a fulfilling personal life. Your organization's success is linked to each individual's psychological needs for growth and accomplishment. Your basic needs are for survival, safety and security, social activity and a sense of belonging, having self-esteem and status, and self-realization and fulfillment. According to psychologist, Abraham Maslow, this "Hierarchy of Needs" is the basic premise of human motivation. You are motivated by the desire to satisfy your needs that are not fully satisfied.

In an Anthony Robbins seminar I attended, the speaker referred to six reasons why people do things as the "Six Human Needs." Although this list is not hierarchical, the top four needs are fundamental human needs whereas numbers five and six are key needs for a fulfilling life. The six needs are:

1. Certainty (comfort)
2. Uncertainty (variety)
3. Significance
4. Love and connection
5. Growth (evolving as a human being)
6. To contribute

To create balance between your company's needs and your own needs, you may need to adjust some of your work habits, attitudes, or behaviors. By changing these behaviors, you are creating more power for your self. Avoid ineffective behaviors by eliminating your need to:

- Please everyone.
- Be liked by everyone.
- Be a super-star at the expense of your life.
- Do everything perfectly.
- Do everything yourself.

Base your behaviors and actions on your values and principles (see Tip #18). Changing behaviors takes courage, commitment, and persistence. Rather than conforming to perceived standards, look for ways to drop some balls you are juggling. Be willing to say "no" to something you would normally agree to (see Tip #21). Prioritize your work and let your boss know if you have too many "top priorities." Focus on being more productive and focused during your workday so that you can leave on time with the knowledge that your work is complete for the day (see Tip #71).

Related Activity: Begin by asking yourself how you can change your behavior at work in order to achieve a greater sense of balance in your life. Start out slowly by making small changes and be willing to take some risks in order to reclaim your life. Change just one behavior at a time so that it is not overwhelming. Get your needs met in more healthy ways.

Recommended Resources

1. *Finding Time: How Corporations, Individuals, And Families Can Benefit From New Work Practices* by Leslie A. Perlow (Cornell University Press, 1997)
2. *His Needs, Her Needs: Building An Affair-Proof Marriage (15th Anniversary)* by Willard F. Harley (Revell, Fleming H. Company, 2001)
3. *The Time Bind: When Work Becomes Home And Home Becomes Work* by Arlie Russell Hochschild (Henry Holt & Company, Inc., 1997

> *Sometimes it is extremely good for you to forget that there is anything in the world that needs to be done, and to do some particular thing that you want to do.*
>
> *~ Eleanor Roosevelt*

TIP # 53 - DE-STRESS BEFORE RETURNING HOME FROM WORK

Easing the re-entry home from a hectic workday is extremely important for you and your family. Leave your stress where it originates. Don't take work stress home or home stress to work—both are ineffective.

Although it may not be the first time you've seen some of these tips, perhaps this will be the first time you actually act on them. Be open to new ideas...any of these tips will improve the transition between work and home if you are serious about decompressing.

- Before you leave work for the day, make a list of the things you'll have to handle tomorrow.
- Immediately upon entering your home, change from work clothes into clothes that help you feel more comfortable.
- Exercise for 15–30 minutes either by yourself or with family members who want to join in.
- Use your commute time as an opportunity to unwind from the day.
- Meditate for at least 15 minutes either before entering your home or in a quiet room once inside.
- Alleviate traffic on your way home by taking a small detour.
- If you take mass transit in a safe area, get off the bus/train one stop prior to your regular and walk the distance, if possible.
- Sit quietly and watch the news or read the newspaper while everyone re-acclimates into the home environment.
- Take a quick shower or bath.
- Put out a healthy snack of cheese and crackers, fresh fruits, or raw vegetables right away so you can relax and serve dinner a little later.
- Tune into your favorite music or inspirational tape.

Related Activity: The next time you find yourself overly stressed out from a "bad" day at work, select any one of the tips above and implement it immediately. Even if you've used other techniques that have worked successfully for you in the past, try some of those listed from time-to-time to see if there's a difference for you. Different stressors often require different responses.

Recommended Resource

1. *Lighten Up And Enjoy Life More: Everyday Ways To De-Stress Your Lifestyle* by Margaret A. Houk (Judson Press, 1996)
2. *Stress Protection Plan: Everyday Ways To Beat Stress And Enjoy Life* by Suzannah Olivier (Sterling Publishing Company, Inc., 2000)
3. *The Three Career Couple—Her Job, His Job And Their Job Together: Mastering The Fine Art Of Juggling Work, Home And Family* by Marcia Byalick and Linda Saslow, (Peterson's Press, 1993)

Beat Stress and Enjoy Life More!

> *Ulcers are contagious. You can get them from your boss.*
>
> *~ Unknown*

TIP # 54 - DON'T KEEP RE-LIVING YOUR WORK STRESS

The ups and downs of the economy in the last decade are exacerbating stress levels for many working parents. Those with full-time jobs are often working an incredible amount of hours. Those who are out of work are often concerned about being able to take care of their family, finding other work, and paying their bills.

So, why do you re-live the stress of your day when you reunite with your loved ones? Too often, evening conversations are spent rehashing the terrible things that happened during the day. You come home after a rough day at work and talk about how many demands were placed on you, the irritating people you faced, the bad experiences you encountered, and other work-related issues. A terrible day should not be re-created in the evening when you reconnect with your family. Re-living the problems from the day does nothing to support your well-being or your family's.

By retelling the horrible experiences you encountered during the day, you are actually going to re-experience them. You wind up draining your energy and validating the negative aspects of your day. Commiserating with others about your difficulties has a high emotional price.

Begin letting go of the bad things that happen during the day rather than rehashing and re-living them again later in the evening. Instead, focus your energy on those things that went well and possible *solutions* for the problems you encounter; be a model for your family by focusing on the positive aspects of your day and those things you have the power to change. Save the discussions about your bad days to share occasionally, not regularly. If sharing the gloomy details really does no good, then give your family a break! However, if discussing the issues helps you de-stress, find other means for blowing off this steam (e.g., journaling, talking it over with a work colleague) so that you don't put too much of a drain on your family.

Related Activity: Become more aware of the conversations you have with your family about your workday and break the habit of dwelling on all the bad stuff that happens. Begin to focus on some of the more positive aspects of your work and see how it makes a difference. If you get into the healthier habit of taking half the energy you use to moan, groan, or complain and direct it into achieving your hopes and desires, your life will begin to look completely different!

Recommended Resources

1. *Coming Up For Air: How To Build A Balanced Life In A Workaholic World* by Beth Sawi (Hyperion, 2000)
2. *Harvard Business Review On Work And Life Balance (Harvard Business Review Paperback Series)* by Harvard Business Review (Harvard Business School, 2000)
3. *Relax–You May Have Only A Few Minutes Left: Using The Power Of Humor To Overcome Stress In Your Life And Work* by Loretta Laroche (Villard Books, 1998)
4. *The One Minute Manager Balances Work And Life (One Minute Manager Library)* by Kenneth H. Blanchard (William Morrow & Company, 1999)
5. *The Pleasure Prescription: To Love, To Work, To Play Life In the Balance* by Paul Pearsall (Hunter House, 1996)
6. *Working Mothers 101: How To Organize Your Life, Your Children, And Your Career To Stop Feeling Guilty And Start Enjoying It All* by Katherine Wyse Goldman (Harper Perennial, 1998)

Working Mothers

TIP # 55 - KNOW YOUR RIGHTS DURING PREGNANCY AND PARENTHOOD

Many of the laws and company policies surrounding maternity rights and benefits can be confusing. Find out as much as possible about what you are personally entitled to. Many of the entitlements vary depending on the length of your employment, who you work for, and where you live. To learn more about what your entitlements might be, contact your human resources or personnel manager, trade union representative, or your local job center or benefits agency (you'll probably be able to find the phone number in your telephone directory). You can also research current legislation using your library or the Internet.

Under much of the current legislation in the US (and many other counties), employers must take reasonable measures to protect all of their employees, including new and expectant mothers, (regardless of their length of service). Employers are responsible to prevent exposure to any risks by removing hazards and implementing controls. Risks to expectant mothers and their babies may include exposure to hazardous chemicals, lifting heavy objects, shocks, vibrations, night work, manual handling of loads, excessive travel, heights, extremes of hot or cold, and working with certain biological agents. When a risk exists, your employer is required to take steps to remove it or make arrangements so you are no longer exposed to it. If they can't remedy the situation, they must make temporary changes in your working conditions or offer you more suitable alternative work. If none of these options are possible, you may be suspended with full pay under the guidelines of the law.

Legislation may also exist to protect you from sex discrimination. Under this legislation, you are not permitted to be unfairly treated (e.g., making your working conditions less favorable than the conditions of your colleagues) or dismissed due to your pregnancy. Employers may also be required to provide suitable facilities for pregnant women or breastfeeding mothers to rest.

Look into the amount of maternity or paternity leave you are eligible to take based on legislation in your country, state, and locality—it normally varies. In some cases the leave is unpaid and in most cases there is a guaranteed reinstatement to a similar position. You may also be eligible for disability and family care leave. It's important to know your rights and benefits. Federal or state legislation sets forth the minimum that you should be eligible for. Your employer may offer additional benefits, so be sure to check with your benefits office to see what you may be entitled to.

Related Activity: Learn your rights and entitlements under current law and employer policies that govern you.

Recommended Resources

1. *Everything A Working Mother Needs To Know About Pregnancy Rights, Maternity Leave, And Making Her Career Work For Her* by Carol A. Buckler and Anne Cicero Weisberg (Main Street Books, 1994)
2. *Working And Caring* by T. Berry Brazelton (Perseus Publishing, 1992)
3. *Working Woman's Baby Planner* by Marla Schram Schwartz (Prentice Hall Professional Technical Reference, 1993)

Maternity is on the face of it an unsociable experience. The selfishness that a woman has learned to stifle or to dissemble where she alone is concerned, blooms freely and unashamed on behalf of her offspring.

~ Emily James Putnam

TIP # 56 - SHARE YOUR NEWS WHEN YOU ARE READY

You might be nervous about telling your employer that you are expecting; you are not legally obligated to tell them until you are ready to do so. Once you choose to tell your boss your news, you will be entitled to special rights like time off for prenatal care, health and safety protection, and protection from dismissal or unfair treatment because of your pregnancy.

Before telling your boss about your pregnancy, be sure to find out what your maternity rights are under current legislation and your company's policies (see Tip #55). Then select when and how you want to share your news. It's usually best to request a meeting at a time when your boss is reasonably relaxed and receptive. After the meeting, there may be specific actions for you and/or your boss to take that is required by law or policy. It is important to follow these guidelines or regulations.

Although your boss may be personally delighted for you, your pregnancy poses many challenges for her; your boss will need to consider the implications of your maternity leave. You will probably be temporarily replaced—which means finding the money, a suitable person, and training him to fill in during your absence.

Related Activity: Keep yourself well-informed about your rights, stay calm, treat issues as you would any other professional matters, and be prepared for ungracious responses to your new situation. Unfortunately, not everyone will be thrilled with your news. Stay healthy and follow your doctor's orders throughout your pregnancy.

> *A mother's heart is always with her children.*
>
> ~ *Chinese Proverb*

TIP # 57 - HANDLE YOUR PREGNANCY AT WORK

When you are having a low-risk, normal pregnancy and work in a safe environment, you can normally continue working for most of your pregnancy.

Morning sickness or nausea is prevalent in 60–90% of pregnant women. This can affect you at work and at home. If you are prone to vomiting, rather than just feeling nauseous, prepare yourself with wipes, mouthwash, water, a change of clothes, and some crackers. If you haven't shared your news at work yet (see Tip #56), you could use other excuses for your vomiting for a while; eventually your colleagues will probably figure things out (frequent trips to the women's restroom, sudden weight gain, and the avoidance of alcohol after work are pretty good "hints!"). If you are suffering from severe or prolonged morning sickness, you may need to tell your supervisor about your pregnancy earlier than you initially planned.

As your pregnancy progresses, the early symptoms of nausea usually subside. You begin "showing" and have difficulty fitting into your regular clothes. Fortunately, business maternity wear is more readily available now and there's more clothing choices you can wear to continue looking professional.

Toward the third trimester (and often in the first, as well) you may experience tiredness, absent-mindedness, and daydreaming. During the second trimester, many expectant moms feel more energetic and focused. Reach out to other new moms who know and understand what you're going through. In many larger companies, support groups for working parents exist and you may get additional support by participating in their meetings.

Decide whether to be private or open about your pregnancy. Some expectant moms welcome and enjoy the opportunities to talk about their pregnancy. Others prefer to keep their pregnancy as a part of their personal life—you get to decide! You get to create the boundaries and handle comments as you see fit. If people touch your belly or make comments you find uncomfortable, be sure to let them know that you'd rather they didn't.

Related Activity: As you continue working during your pregnancy, it's important that you take good care of yourself. Do what you can to increase your comfort and keep both you and your baby healthy and safe. Some examples of how you can take care of yourself include:

- Slightly elevate your feet to keep the circulation moving.
- Dress comfortably and wear comfy shoes and maternity hose, if necessary.
- Stretch your body every now and then.
- Drink plenty of water regularly; avoid caffeine.
- Eat healthily.
- Use the restroom whenever it's necessary.
- Be aware of risks to you and your baby and take the necessary precautions.
- Take breaks and rest when you can.
- Reduce or eliminate stress factors.
- Seek out and accept help.
- Follow your doctor's orders.

Recommended Resources

1. *Pregnancy For Dummies* by Joanne Stone and Mary Murray (John Wiley & Sons, Inc., 1999)
2. *The Girlfriends' Guide To Pregnancy: Or Everything Your Doctor Won't Tell You* by Vicki Iovine (Simon & Schuster, 1995)
3. *The Good Housekeeping Illustrated Book Of Pregnancy And Baby Care* by Ellen Levine (Editor) (Hearst Books, 2001)
4. *What To Expect When You're Expecting (Revised)* by Heidi Murkoff (Workman Publishing Company, Inc., 2002)

> *Don't worry. With some advance planning, it is possible to successfully combine work and breastfeeding*
> *~ Kathleen B. Bruce (RN, BSN, IBCLC)*

TIP # 58 - COMBINE WORK AND BREASTFEEDING

If you've been breastfeeding your baby, it is well worth the effort to continue after you return to work even though you'll be faced with many challenges. It will require commitment and work if you are determined to continue to breastfeed (but many mothers believe it is worth it to provide the best possible nourishment for their baby).

Although many working mothers used to nurse for a few weeks and then wean before they returned to work, these days moms often continue to nurse after they return to work, too. There are several important elements to consider in order to successfully nurse your baby when you return to work. It's advisable to gradually transition back to work so you and your baby can adapt.

Several options exist for mothers who choose to continue breastfeeding. If your childcare provider is located close enough to your workplace, take your breaks at regular intervals (about every 3–4 hours is usually sufficient) so that you can go breastfeed your baby. If not, you can use your break time to pump and store your milk. If you are pumping, you will need a refrigerator or cooler to properly store the milk and keep it cold. Lastly, you can breastfeed your baby when you are together and use formula when you are separated. Realize you'll need to adjust your milk supply to accommodate for the longer separation.

If you want to continue breastfeeding after you return to work, you'll need to:

- Choose a childcare provider who supports your commitment to breastfeeding.
- Establish a good milk supply so that you can more easily maintain it.
- Select an appropriate breast pump.

- Arrange breaks at regular intervals during the day in order to have time to pump (or feed your baby).
- Arrange a comfortable private place to pump (preferably with an electric outlet).
- Have a place to wash your breast pump after using it.

Although leaking tends to lessen after the early weeks of nursing, leaking at work is much more of a concern than leaking at home. Here are some tips for dealing with leaking problems:

- Cross your arms across your chest and apply pressure for about 10 seconds if you feel your milk letting down at an inopportune moment.
- Wear bright or dark colored prints made of cotton or synthetic fabrics to conceal leaks; white and pastel colors and silks, linens, and clingy fabrics show leaks more.
- Throw a loose jacket, sweater, blazer or scarf over your blouse or keep a neutrally colored spare blouse handy.
- Keep your clothes loose and comfortable. Select outfits that button in front or two-piece outfits that you can easily pull up or out of the way.
- Choose washable clothes that are easy to care for.
- Have an ample and accessible supply of pads available.

It's important to know your rights (see Tip #55). Most governments have enacted some form of legislation protecting the breastfeeding rights of working mothers and have established means for its enforcement. Your physician, lactation consultant, or the La Leche League can help you.

Related Activity: If you are planning on pumping at work, increase your milk supply and create a reserve stock of milk for your initial days at work.

Recommended Resources
(Note: an abundance of sites and information are available about this topic on the Internet. Use your search engine to select a few.)

1. *Breastfeeding And The Working Mother* by Diane Mason (St. Martin's Press, Inc., 1997)
2. *Breastfeeding Success For Working Mothers* by Marilyn Grams and Itoko Takeuchi (Achievement Press, 1985)
3. *Nursing Mother, Working Mother: The Essential Guide For Breastfeeding And Staying Close To Your Baby After You Return To Work* by Gale Pryor (Harvard Common Press, 1997)
4. *The Maternity Leave Breastfeeding Plan: How To Enjoy Nursing For 3 Months And Go Back To Work Guilt*-Free by William G. Wilkoff (Simon & Schuster Trade Paperbacks, 2002)

Breastfeeding is a Natural & Healthy Way to Nourish Your Baby!

> *While aimlessly waiting for their so-called "ship" to come in and change their life for the better, far too many people miss the boat that could actually carry them to a brighter future. They are often so afraid of testing new waters that they spend an entire lifetime waiting on the shore. Begin your journey now!*
>
> *~ Josh Hinds*

TIP # 59 - PREPARE TO TRANSITION BACK TO WORK

Regardless of when you choose to return to work, it is often a difficult decision and one that requires some mental and emotional adjustments. This tip will help you make the transition from being a stay-at-home parent to being a working parent. In deciding to resume your career, you'll also need to consider whether you'd like to return to your previous career or seek out a new area of interest.

Begin by assessing what you really want to do in your work life. What skills, talents, opportunities, and resources are available to you? What do you value? What do you need? Why do you want to work? What motivates and energizes you at work?

Now that you've had some time away from your career, you may decide that a change is in order. It's possible that the career you had before you had children is too demanding or requires too much travel now that you have a family. Perhaps you've discovered new hobbies you'd like to pursue as a career. You might like to receive additional training in an area of interest and may elect to take some classes. Maybe temporary employment will help you bridge the gap and help you get used to working again outside the home. Part-time employment may also work well to help ease the transition back to work or as a work alternative.

Begin by describing your "ideal" job with as much specificity as possible (e.g., What kind of work environment? What sorts of people? How do you want to contribute? How long is your commute? What types and sizes of companies are you interested in? What hours would you like to work? What skills do you want to use? Who is your customer? Are you interested in self-employment? What types of businesses would you like to pursue owning?) Once you have a clear idea of what you would like to do and where, you can begin researching prospective employers (or business opportunities) to see how they stand up to your criteria.

Even if you've only taken a short break, if you're going back to the same career you may be quite surprised by some of the changes that have taken place during your absence. Hopefully, you've stayed abreast of the changes in your field. If not, it may be time for some cramming to make yourself marketable again. So catch up on what's been going on, read up on industry news in professional trade journals and other sources, and talk to people in your network. Raise your self-esteem and self-confidence by strengthening your skills and focusing on your past accomplishments.

As you create your resume, consider using a functional style format rather than a chronological resume. A functional resume highlights your work history in a summative form. In your resume and job interviews make only unapologetic positive statements about the gap in your employment for full-time parenting, explaining that you took time off to raise your family.

To prepare for the transition, begin eliminating stuff from your life that doesn't support you, like negative people and clutter (see Tip #13). Arrange for adequate childcare. Build a network of supportive resources and people. Realize that it will be necessary to keep things in perspective; let go of your standards of *perfection* and replace them with more realistic standards that are *good enough*. Set clear boundaries (see Tip #19) and be willing to say "no" to the many requests for your time and other resources (see Tip #21). Be flexible, open-minded and above all, have a sense of humor!

Related Activity: Use a gradual approach to start preparing yourself (emotionally, physically, and mentally) to transition back to work. Choose a childcare provider that you and your child are comfortable with and begin the routine that would mimic your work schedule a week or more before you return to work on a regular basis. Help your caregiver get to know your child's idiosyncrasies, their likes and dislikes, favorite things, comfort items, and routines. Never sneak away without saying good-bye to your child. If your child gets emotional and clingy on good-byes allow extra time but depart as quickly as possible. Reconnect with your child in a warm comfortable manner when you return to pick him up.

Remember that your working outside the home will be an adjustment for everyone. Be patient with yourself and others as you establish new routines and learn to adjust appropriately!

Recommended Resource

Life's Work: Confessions Of An Unbalanced Mom by Lisa Belkin (Simon & Schuster Adult Publishing Group, 2002)

You Can Succeed as a Working Mother!

Career Satisfaction

> *There is no future in any job. The future is in the man who holds the job.*
>
> ~ *Author Unknown*

TIP # 60 - TAKE CHARGE OF YOUR CAREER

Loving your work opens the door to loving your whole life. Think of your work as if it were your own company (regardless of whether or not you are self-employed). Continue adding to your credentials, skills, knowledge, experience, and competencies as if you were preparing for an IPO (Initial Public Offering). Imagine making yourself so valuable that you are at your mastery level, headhunters are tearing down your door, and companies are having bidding wars to get you—wouldn't it be pretty cool to have so many options to choose from! You'll have to do this for yourself; no employer will do it for you.

Related Activity: Review your career portfolio, trends within the industry and your passions. Create a career plan that's aligned with who you are and what's truly important to you. Get on-track with where you want to be by getting extra training, volunteering for specific opportunities, and meeting new people within and outside your current company. There are many worthwhile books, Web sites, career coaches and career counselors if you need extra help.

Recommended Resources

1. *Career Choice, Change & Challenge: 125 Strategies From The Experts At CareerJournal.com* by Deb Koen and Tony Lee (Jist Publishing, Inc., 2000)
2. *Do What You Are: Discover The Perfect Career For You Through The Secrets Of Personality Type—Revised And Updated Edition Featuring E-careers For the 21st Century* by

Paul D. Tieger and Barbara Barron-Tieger (Little Brown & Company, 2001)

3. *Do What You Love For The Rest Of Your Life: A Practical Guide To Career Change And Personal Renewal* by Bob Griffiths (Ballantine Publishing Group, 2001)

4. *The New Quick Job-Hunting Map: How To Create A Picture Of Your Ideal Job Or Next Career* by Richard Nelson Bolles (Ten Speed Press, 1990)

5. *The Pathfinder: How To Choose Or Change Your Career For A Lifetime Of Satisfaction And Success* by Nicholas Lore (Fireside, 1998)

6. *What Color Is Your Parachute? A Practical Manual For Job-Hunters & Career Changers* by Richard Nelson Bolles (Ten Speed Press, 2002)

7. *What Every Successful Woman Knows: 12 Breakthrough Strategies To Get The Power And Ignite Your Career* by Janice Reals Ellig and Bill Morin (McGraw-Hill Professional, 2001)

Attain Career Satisfaction!

> *Choose a job you love, and you will never have to work a day in your life.*
>
> *~ Confucius*

TIP # 61 - DO WORK THAT YOU LOVE

Work comprises a major portion of your time away from your family and should, therefore, be fulfilling to you. You spend more time working than doing anything else—an average of 150,000 hours over a lifetime. That's why it's important to know *why* you work. In a recent study by the *Rockport Institute*, only 10% of Americans said they love their work—that it's fun, challenging, and a significant source of personal growth; that they view their work as the ultimate expression of a clear and meaningful purpose. However, another 70% of Americans go to work daily without much enthusiasm or passion for their work and the other 20% are somewhere in between.

If you look at your work, is it based on a *should*? As you've probably come to see by now, "should's" are those rules that were unconsciously programmed into you about what you're supposed to be, do, or have. Your parents, schools, society, religion, and your friends set these expectations. These beliefs are deeply rooted and often permeate your thoughts. Unfortunately, they can significantly limit your potential. The good news is that when you *recognize* a "should" in your life, this belief can be refocused to something that reveals more possibilities for you and launches you into greater career satisfaction. Begin weeding out those "should's" and focus instead on what you really want.

Look to have your work support your values. When you are doing work that is aligned with your values you feel most like yourself. Your work becomes a source of energy, joy, and fulfillment. When your work is not aligned with your values, you naturally feel frustrated, bored, or wanting something more. Personally fulfilling work allows you to express and honor your values.

When you love your work you look forward to life, have heightened self-esteem, enjoy better health and a longer life, and you are more fun to be around.

Related Activity: Stop settling for a standard of fulfillment in your work life that is considerably lower than what is really possible. Ask yourself whether or not you really like your work. If you don't like your work, make a decision to stop settling and take actions to create more fulfillment. Take a few minutes to remind yourself why you do what you do. What's the compelling reason?

Recommended Resources

1. *Do What You Love, The Money Will Follow: Discovering Your Right Livelihood* by Marsha Sinetar (Dell Publishing Company, Inc., 1989)
2. *Doing Work You Love: Discovering Your Purpose And Realizing Your Dreams* by Cheryl Gilman (Barnes & Noble Books, 2002)
3. *Finding Your Perfect Work: The New Career Guide To Making A Living, Creating A Life* by Paul and Sarah Edwards (J.P.Tarcher, 1996)
4. *How To Do What You Love For A Living* by Nancy Anderson (Fine Communications, 1999)
5. *I Could Do Anything If I Only Knew What It Was: How To Discover What You Really Want And How To Get It* by Barbara Sher (Dell Publishing Company, 1995)
6. *Making A Life, Making A Living: Reclaiming Your Purpose And Passion In Business And In Life* by Mark Albion (Warner Books, 2000)

> *You don't get to choose how you're going to die, or when. You can only decide how you're going to live. Now.*
>
> ~ *Joan Baez*

TIP # 62 - STOP OVERWORKING

Many people work a tremendous amount of hours due to a decreasing work force, budget cuts, a fluctuating economy, technology, and their own inability to set limits. Overworking is a growing problem that you can do something about if you are ready to make some changes and take control of your work.

In addition to your job you still have responsibilities at home. Instead of feeling like a sanctuary, your home and your children often end up feeling like another burden or assignment that you need to deal with. Your home life might feel like a second job and work never seems to end. Take note...you and your family are at risk when you work around-the-clock.

Unfortunately, the tendency to overwork hits moms exceedingly hard because most are working more intensely than their spouse does (if you have one) during the hours away from the office. Now, for you dads out there, realize that it's critically important for the overall health and well being of your wife and family that you pitch in extra around the house. (And, if you are already a saint of a dad and spouse and offended by my comments, please accept my apology and realize that I'm referring to the majority of men, but certainly not all!)

Some companies are redesigning the structure of work processes, where possible, to cut hours and reduce stress. If you are a manager or business owner, you can stop expecting overwork to be the norm and you can start establishing more reasonable expectations Contrary to what you might believe, overworked employees are not loyal and would probably leave the company the first chance they get. Overworked employees feel miserable, unappreciated, rushed, and extremely stressed out. Working longer hours does not make anyone more productive! It's important to take better care of your employees; the price tag for replacing an employee who quits normally runs several times their salary—and their loyalty is priceless!

141

If you are an employee, you can begin taking control of your life and making the most efficient use of your work time. You can also begin setting boundaries (see Tip #19) and saying "no" (see Tip #21) more often at work. The general nature of working women is to nurture others and to take on too much work for fear of possible repercussions. The way you are socialized from an early age contributes greatly to your inability to say "no". Working moms often walk around feeling guilty that they don't do enough at work or at home. The inability to say "no" at work means that you carry an extra load of stress which can result in health issues, including digestive problems, sleep disturbances, depression, or anxiety disorders. Begin applying yourself more strategically instead of taking on everything that comes your way. Look at each new task or project and consciously determine those you wish to handle. Stop saying "yes" without thinking.

Be willing to turn away from all the available technology if you really want a break from work. With today's technology you can constantly be in touch with the office. You are never "off" work. As a result, work is nonstop. Even when you are home with your family, you are still closely connected to work if you never shut off the beeper, cell phone, and laptop to fully focus on your family.

Working too many hours jeopardizes your family life and your health. It can also affect the quality of your work. You will continue suffering from overwork unless you are willing to make a firm decision to stop.

Related Activity: Take responsibility for your life. Stop sacrificing the quality of your life and stop putting such high demands on yourself. When your body breaks down because you're pushing too hard, everything will come to a crashing halt. Take control now—don't wait for an emergency or disaster to occur.

Recommended Resource

Get Your Act Together: A 7-Day Get-Organized Program For The Overworked, Overbooked, And Overwhelmed by Pam Young and Peggy Jones (Harper Collins Publishers,1993)

> *To give anything less than your best is to sacrifice the gift.*
> ~ *Steve Prefontaine*

TIP # 63 - BE A VALUED CONTRIBUTOR

To have any chance of success in creating the work and life you want, it's critical to make sure that you really are a top-notch performer. At work, you are responsible for your own career success. Being responsible requires you to be flexible and adaptable. Whether you own your own business or are employed by others, you have "customers." Your customers are the people you deliver products or services to. They could be your boss, a colleague, a client, a patient, or the organization. Regardless of who your customers are, when you treat them as a customer, you focus on delivering results that exceed expectations. This is what adds value!

You can increase your value by being conscientious about the work you perform, by focusing on completing the task at hand in a high quality manner, and by communicating clearly to others.

Although few jobs are safe when companies are forced to make budget cuts, when you're a valued contributor you're less likely to be arbitrarily dismissed. If you've been a good employee and performed beyond expectations, it will set you apart from others, thus making you more valuable to the organization. In some cases, a valued contributor will be reassigned to a new position and saved from a layoff. Unfortunately, in other cases, the quality of your work and your contributions are not taken into account when layoff decisions are made but are reflected in letters of recommendation, referrals, and new opportunities.

At a minimum, you should be aware of where you stand in your present job and you should begin modifying your style and behavior to ensure your boss knows that you are "on task" and contributing to the organization's goals. Assess yourself to determine whether the work you do makes a difference for the company. How do you contribute to the bottom line (qualitatively and quantitatively)?

Review your last performance assessment or notes from your most recent goal-setting meeting with your boss. Set up a time to talk with your boss to ensure that your contributions continue to align with the larger goals of the organization. To be a successful contributor and a valued employee, you always need to know what is important today *and* in the future. Know your organization's goals and purposes so that you can help to achieve them.

With change an active part of everyday life, your business goals and objectives are much less likely to remain solid. They change to adapt to the business and customer requirements of your market. You're ability to adapt, remain flexible, and to learn new tools, concepts, or techniques will increase your value to your organization. Continue your personal and professional growth.

Related Activity: Keep a file of your accomplishments and successes, including your performance evaluations, letters of recommendation, and your own descriptions of difficult and challenging situations where you performed well. Also include customer feedback. Refer to this file whenever you begin to doubt your competence *and* at appropriate times when speaking to others about additional opportunities.

Recommended Resource

1. *1001 Ways To Take Initiative At Work* by Bob Nelson (Workman Publishing Company, Inc,. 1999)
2. *Fish! Tales: Real Life Stories To Help You Transform Your Workplace And Your Life* by Stephen C. Lundin and John Christensen (Hyperion Press, 2002)
3. *Please Don't Just Do What I Tell You!: Do What Needs To Be Done: Every Employee's Guide To Making Work More Rewarding* by Bob B. Nelson with Ken Blanchard (Hyperion Press, 2001)
4. *Zap The Gaps!: Target Higher Performance And Achieve It!* by Ken H. Blanchard and James C. Robinson (William Morrow & Company, 2002)

> *Never continue in a job you don't enjoy. If you're happy in what you're doing, you'll like yourself, you'll have inner peace. And if you have that, along with physical health, you will have had more success than you could possibly have imagined.*
>
> ~ *Rodan of Alexandria*

TIP # 64 - SURVIVE A LAYOFF

The US Labor Report continuously announced job losses during the first months of the 21st century and for the months preceding. Layoffs, downsizings, rightsizings (or whatever name they go by) result in voluntary and involuntary cuts from the workforce. To the working parent, being told that you're about to be the next cut can offer a full range of emotions from fear about how you will contribute to your family's financial needs, to elation that you are now forced to find a new career that is more fulfilling to you, or ambivalence about the opportunity to take some time off to devote to your family. When you are in the position to voluntarily leave (with an enhanced benefits and/or early retirement package), you are faced with a number of decisions that impact you, your future, your children, and your spouse, as well. Just remember, your career is a part of your life—it's not your whole life!

Be aware of the signs of a possible impending layoff at your company. Watch for:

- hiring freezes
- spending warnings
- project cancellations
- negative news articles
- low quotas
- fewer customer installations
- budget cuts or expense reductions
- travel cutbacks
- restructuring
- management resignations
- termination of temporary employees and contractors
- attrition without replacement hiring

- reductions in support staff
- or, if your company's competitors, suppliers, or customers are laying off, because it's quite likely that your company will too, especially if economic conditions are effecting your industry.

If only a few of these signs exist, there may be nothing to worry about. However, if you see more (especially along the lines of hiring freezes, budget cuts, restructuring, and layoffs in your industry), it might be a good time to get your resume up-to-date, start networking, and begin looking for a new job. If the possibility seems inevitable, implement measures to build a financial reserve so that you have more time and flexibility on your side.

If you do get laid off, don't forget that you have job skills and many strengths to offer. You probably also have more opportunities than you initially think you have. Rather than jumping quickly into another job, take some time to assess what you really want to be doing, where the trends for jobs are today and in the future and take some training to enhance your skills, if necessary. Begin by taking at least a few days to evaluate your situation. Ask yourself the following questions: What type of new position am I looking for? How does this fit in with my long-term career goals? What type of company would I like to work for? What skills do I currently have? What new skills would I like to learn? Who are the potential employers in the area? Where, if anywhere am I willing to relocate?

Searching for a new job often becomes a full-time job in itself, but don't forget to find ways to keep a balance in your life during your quest. Time for renewal contributes to your creativity, health and energy, and helps you avoid burning out.

Related Activity: If you know you're going to quit or think you might be getting fired or laid off soon, prepare now by doing the following:

- Take your personal property home (so there's no question about what belongs to you or the company on your last day).
- Remove personal items (software, e-mails, etc.) from your computer.

- Collect contact information from your associates for future references, potential networking, and vendors and clients, if appropriate.
- Get letters of recommendation (be sure they explain that the job loss wasn't your fault).
- Begin networking, especially outside the company.
- Compile a portfolio of your work.
- Review your financial situation and create a budget.
- Update your resume, post it on-line, and be sure to get it into the hands of others who might be able to help you.
- Take advantage of any outplacement services your company offers.
- Be ready to negotiate with human resources, or your boss, for more money or a better severance package.
- If you're interested in staying with the company, ask your human resource's representative and other colleagues about jobs in other departments where your skills may be transferable.
- To avoid excessive worry, keep your mind busy in your free time and make yourself useful by working on your house, car, yard, garden, hobbies, and other activities. But also, allow yourself to experience the natural feelings that occur in your situation and let others support you.
- Communicate with those around you, especially your family.
- Realize that being laid off, or having the opportunity to leave with a voluntary severance package, can end up being the best thing that ever happened to you. It may be the perfect chance for the career change, training, or self-employment that you've been contemplating but never seemed to have the time or courage to pursue.

Recommended Resources

1. *Answers From Within: Spiritual Guidelines For Managing Setbacks In Work And Life* by William J. Byron (Hungry Minds Inc., 1998)
2. *Career Bounce-Back: Professionals In Transition Guide To Recovery & Reemployment* by J. Damian Birkel, Stacey J. Miller (Amacon, 1997)
3. *Dare To Change Your Job And Your Life* by Carole Kanchier, PhD (Jist Works, 2000)
4. *Fired With Enthusiasm II: A Take-Charge Game Plan For A Quick Career Comeback* by Tom Lonergan (Authors Choice Press, 2002)
5. *Reinventing Your Career: Surviving A Layoff & Creating New Opportunities* by Stephen B. Adams (Northfield Publishers, 1996)
6. *Surviving A Layoff: Managing Stress, Family And Finances—Discovering New Opportunities And New Potential—How To Package, Market And Sell Yourself—Tips For Starting* by Harry S. Dahlstrom (Dahlstrom & Company, 1998)

Losing Your Job Offers New Beginnings

Work Alternatives

> *We must look for ways to be an active force in our own lives. We must take charge of our own destinies, design a life of substance and truly begin to live our dreams.*
>
> ~ Les Brown

TIP # 65 - NEGOTIATE ALTERNATIVE WORK ARRANGEMENTS

Some of the most popular alternative work arrangements include working part-time, telecommuting (or working from home), job-sharing, flexible scheduling, and working as an independent contractor. Each tip in this *Work Alternatives* section will help you explore the different arrangement possibilities in more detail.

If your organization has family-friendly programs and policies that provide flexibility in how, when, where, and how often you work, why not *negotiate* for what you need? Companies like this create opportunities for employees to meet personal responsibilities while still being productive on-the-job.

If your organization has been slow to adopt these policies and perks, research what other (preferably similar) companies are doing and provide this information to your boss and/or the human resources department. Discuss your suggestions regarding how these policies and perks might work within your organization based on its culture and environment. Focus mostly on the benefits the organization may derive as a result of becoming more family-friendly.

Look at the trends within your organization. Do women end up leaving after they have a baby? Are managers inflexible or intolerant of outside needs? Why are people leaving? Is there a high turnover rate? It's very costly for organizations to replace a valuable employee so many organizations have adopted flexible work arrangement options to reduce their turnover rate and increase employee retention and loyalty.

Related Activity: Once you've gotten your organization open to flexible work arrangements, determine what would work best for you. Draw up a proposal that outlines how the work will get done and the benefits to the company. Then, present your proposal to your boss. Be clear with your alternatives if they do not accept your plan but don't be threatening. If they don't accept, you can decide whether to continue working there under the same conditions, re-negotiate other suitable arrangements, find a job in a more family-friendly environment, leave the workforce, start your own business, or ????

Be willing to establish a trial period for a specified number of months if your boss or employer is hesitant about the plan. Check-in frequently and be prepared to adjust in order to make it work.

Recommended Resources

1. See www.workoptions.com/ for a *Flex Success Proposal Blueprint* and some related articles. Pat Katepoo shares practical advice, negotiating tips, and some real-world strategies that have helped others get the flexible work arrangements they wanted.
2. *Creating A Flexible Workplace: How To Select And Manage Alternative Work Options* by Barney Olmsted and Suzanne Smith (Amacom, 1994)
3. *Flex Appeal: An Inspirational Guide To Flexible Work For Mothers* by Jacqueline Foley (Out Of Our Minds Press, 2002)
4. *Flexible Work Options: A Guidebook For Employees, Managers And Human Resource Professionals* by Kathy-Kane Zweber (Motorola University Press, 1997)
5. *Put Work In Its Place: How You Can Redesign Your Job To Fit Your Life* by Bruce O'Hara (New Star Books, 1994)
6. *Telecommuting Success: A Practical Guide For Staying In The Loop While Working Away From The Office* by Michael J. Dziak and Gil Gordon (JIST Works, Inc., 2001)

> *Some workers are trying to make both weekends meet.*
>
> ~ *Unknown*

TIP # 66 - DECIDE IF PART-TIME IS RIGHT FOR YOU

If you could wave a magic wand, would you reduce your workweek and spend more time with your children? If so, spending more time at home may not be as costly as you think. The reduction in work hours and wages would be offset by the opportunity to share more small everyday moments with your children, and your life often becomes relatively easier.

You might want to consider moving from full-time to part-time work. If your present employer doesn't offer part-time options, ask them to consider offering part-time schedules on a trial basis to see how they would work in your environment. If they agree, you should communicate with your boss often in order to ease any concerns about the new working arrangement.

Sometimes, you may be able to transfer to another department within your company that's more amenable to part-time work. However, when part-time is absolutely not an option, you may need to seek employment outside the company if you want to pursue part-time opportunities. When the economy is booming, there are more positions available than employers can fill so they may be more open to this type of arrangement. When things are tight, employers may be open to part-time employees as a cost-saving measure; many employers do not offer (full) benefits to part-time workers.

Part-time workers are often good for business, too. The reduced work schedule increases overall employee morale, raises productivity, and company loyalty. Additionally, there are usually lower rates of absenteeism amongst part-timers.

If you think you are ready to work part-time, consider the pros and cons for both yourself and your employer. Determine how much you need to earn and brainstorm which expenses you can eliminate, such as a weekly housekeeper, an expensive wardrobe budget, or dinners out. Talk with others who are already working part-time to find out their strategy and approach. Compute how much your employer spends on your benefits and other perks that you may be willing to forego. Knowing these facts can make it easier to negotiate.

Analyze your job to determine which aspects can be broken into projects and done by a freelancer or a junior colleague and which responsibilities you want to keep. If your job truly demands full-time coverage, negotiating a job share may be a more suitable option (see Tip #67). Try to make adequate provisions to cut your workload prior to starting with your reduced work schedule and be firm about keeping the arrangement in place, otherwise you might end up working a full-time job in part-time hours with reduced pay and benefits!

When you are ready to speak with your boss about your reduced schedule proposal, be prepared with your plan and be ready to answer her objections. Many bosses have never managed a part-timer and may be concerned at first. Building in a trial period of 3-6 months so you can prove yourself can make the part-time schedule more appealing to your boss. Arrange a formal meeting to discuss your plan. Treat the proposal as a business proposition with potential benefits to both you and your boss. Don't act as if you're asking for a huge favor. Be sure the timing is right for your meeting so that you can openly discuss the issues. Try to reach agreement on the major points first, such as the number of hours you'll work, your adjusted pay rate, and benefits. Be sure to discuss how a part-time schedule might affect your career. Find out if you'll still be eligible for training programs, tuition assistance, and if you'd still be considered for promotion opportunities.

If your part-time proposal is accepted, you'll need to convince your boss and colleagues that the arrangement is working for everyone. Make sure your co-workers know that your intention is not that they wind up picking up the slack because you're working less. Be willing to pitch in extra during extremely busy periods and during crunch times. Although part-timers are normally highly productive and organized, don't stop networking; stay connected with others by occasionally chatting, networking, or having lunch so that you are plugged into the happenings of the company.

Related Activity: Determine if part-time work is a viable option for you. Calculate how a part-time schedule will affect your family's finances. Interestingly, some families find that reduced income and increased cost for benefits are offset by lower childcare and income tax expenses (if you drop down a bracket). Use the worksheet on the following page to help you calculate your costs and savings.

Recommended Resources

1. *Going Part-Time: The Insider's Guide For Professional Women Who Want A Career And A Life* by Cindy Tolliver and Nancy Chambers (Avon Books, 1997)
2. *How To Raise A Family On Less Than Two Incomes—The Complete Guide To Managing Your Money Better So You Can Spend More Time With Your Kids* by Denise Topolnicki (Broadway Books, 2001)

Can You Afford to Work Part-Time?

To Work or Not to Work
(and Everything In-Between)

Financial Analysis

Money You Forfeit:
Income   Change in Dollars
- Salary $_____
- Bonus $_____
- Others $_____

TOTAL DECREASE IN INCOME $_____

Cost of Benefits Replacement
- Medical Coverage $_____
- Disability Insurance $_____
- Life Insurance $_____
- Retirement-Plan Contributions $_____
- Others

TOTAL COST OF BENEFITS $_____

Money You Save:
- Taxes (Federal, State, FICA) $_____
- Transportation (fuel, maintenance, $_____
  train, bus)
- Childcare Expenses $_____
- Meals out (including coffee, soda $_____
  and bottled water on-the-go)
- Professional Wardrobe
  (for purchasing and dry cleaning) $_____
- Hired Housekeeper $_____
- Others $_____

TOTAL EXPENSES SAVED $_____

    Decrease in Income $_____
    + Cost of Benefits $_____
    = Total Dollars Lost $_____
    - Money you Save $_____
    = Actual Shortfall $_____

> *A well-written proposal is the most effective way to get the boss's approval of a flexible work arrangement. That's a time-proven fact.*
>
> ~ *Pat Katepoo*

TIP # 67 - CONSIDER JOB-SHARING

Job-sharing is a viable flexible work option. In a job-share two people share the responsibilities of one full-time position, dividing work, pay, holidays, and other benefits between them according to the time they work. For management, clients, support staff, and peers this team is one entity. Job-sharing enables any role, including senior or managerial positions and administrative or staff positions, to be performed by two separate employees. Job-share members utilize their own skills, experiences, and expertise to enhance the performance of the team.

Job-sharers are synergistic partnerships that are based on communication, commitment, trust, common goals, and complimentary strengths. It takes a solid game plan and constant training to ensure that a job-share team is working at peak performance. When it does, the reputation and performance of the team may far exceed what either individual could have accomplished on their own. Job-sharing offers many solutions to a company's organizational issues, as well as meeting the needs of individual employees.

The position is split to meet the needs of the job-sharers and the job itself. The time may be split in a variety of ways including alternate days of the week or two-and-a-half days each per week. They can also overlap so that the job-sharers can communicate face-to-face or attend important meetings together.

Key benefits of job-sharing for the company and the individuals:

- Job-share partnerships maximize individual strengths while minimizing weaknesses because two people each bring their own set of skills and experience to the job.

155

- Allows for flexibility and continuity because job-sharers can cover for each other when one is unable to work.
- Increases energy and enthusiasm for the work because individual needs can be better met.
- Rewards talent and increases job satisfaction.
- Increases morale and productivity while reducing staff turnover. When an employee has created a more balanced life through job sharing, their anxiety and stress levels are greatly reduced and they tend to stay in a job longer.
- A job-sharing option can be a benefit that is used as an attraction and retention mechanism.

If you are interested in working as part of a job-share team, you can find your partner by networking in your current workplace, in professional networks (e.g., associations or alliances), in your personal networks (e.g., friends, playgroups, or at the gym), in placement offices, employment agencies, and in classified advertisements. Look for a partner who will work with you in a consistent and complimentary manner that allows both of you to minimize your weaknesses and maximize your strengths. Time and persistence can yield several prospective job-share partners.

Once you have selected your job-share partner, the next crucial step is to negotiate the components of your agreement, including your work schedules, benefits, compensation, and communication methods. Remain focused on the responsibilities and deadlines of the position and try not to let your personal agendas conflict with or overshadow the duties of the job. Focus on how you will work together as a team before figuring out when each of you will work. Seek arrangements that are mutually satisfying for the job-share team and your employer.

Related Activity: If a job-share situation seems enticing to you, research it further at one of the Web sites provided on the next page. While investigating for this tip, I found sites in the US, Ireland and the UK that research, develop, and promote job-shares. Find and talk to several job-share teams either inside or outside your current company. Locate potential job-share partners and prepare a proposal and pre-job-share agreement.

Recommended Resources
The following Web sites offer resources and additional information regarding this type of arrangement:

- www.sharegoals.com/home.asp
- www.workoptions.com/jobshare.htm
- www.JobSharing.com
- www.womans-work.com/
- http://iaia.essortment.com/jobsharingprin_oop.htm
- www.jobshare.ie (Ireland)
- www.flexible-recruitment.co.uk/on-line_jobshare_register.html (United Kingdom)

> *Stay committed to your decisions, but stay flexible in your approach.*
> ~ *Tony Robbins*

TIP # 68 - EXPLORE FLEXTIME

Flextime is another alternative work option. It allows you to select the hours you work within specified time limits set by your employer. In some cases, you can work a compressed workweek that consists of four 10–hour days rather than a more "typical" five days, eight hours a day.

Working parents can really benefit from working a flexible or compressed schedule because it allows them greater opportunity to meet the demands of their family. Employers benefit by being able to accommodate their employees who are having difficulty balancing their work and their family without an expense to the company. They can also help increase their customer service hours to cover the staggered schedule with some employees beginning work early and others staying late.

Flextime may be an ideal solution as part of your work and family balance strategy. It can be the easiest flexible work arrangement to negotiate and have approved at work. You request a starting and ending time that accommodates your needs within set limits by your employer. For instance, if you normally work 8:00 a.m.–5:00 p.m., in your flextime schedule you might work 6:00 a.m.–3:00 p.m. or 9:00 a.m.–6:00 p.m.

Once you have your schedule approved, be prepared for possible resentment from co-workers, misunderstandings from customers, a need to communicate your new schedule, and the need to establish limits on your nonworking time (while offering some degree of flexibility to meet the needs of the business). Although a written proposal is often unnecessary with this work option, if you submit a proposal to your employer that details how the new schedule will improve productivity it may help alleviate concerns. Meet periodically with your boss to make sure the schedule is really working; you can reconfigure your schedule as needed before bigger problems arise. Anticipate the needs of your family and your work, and plan accordingly. Remember that working a flexible work schedule is a privilege and not a right. Be sure to honor your agreements with your employer and show up on time, work productively, and don't leave before your agreed-upon quitting time.

Related Activity: Determine a work schedule that would accommodate your personal and work needs. Discuss your proposal with your boss, create a written proposal, and submit it if necessary.

Recommended Resource

Gender, Time And Reduced Work by Cynthia Negrey (State University of New York Press, 1993)

Discover the Work Arrangement that Works for You!

> *There are two primary choices in life: to accept conditions as they exist, or accept the responsibility for changing them.*
>
> *~ Dr. Denis Waitley*

TIP # 69 - WORK FROM HOME

Every day more and more people are choosing to find work-at-home jobs. In the past, the majority of people doing this were moms who wanted to be home with their children. That's changing now because more moms and dads are looking for ways to earn a good income from home with either full- or part-time work. Fact is, it can be a challenge and a bit frustrating to find work that is enjoyable and fits your personality and income requirements, as well as your skill level. Equally challenging is the need to establish distinct workspace, manage time, and balance the needs of demanding clients with equally demanding children. If you find your niche and confront and handle the challenges then working from home may be the best solution for you.

There are actually three different forms of home employment: telecommuting, a home-based job, and a home-based business. In telecommuting, you're still an employee, but your employer allows you to work from home several days a week. This tip focuses exclusively on home-based jobs and home-based business options.

In a home-based job you're working for a company, but they consider you to be an independent contractor and not an employee. The company contracts you to complete certain projects in a given time frame or handle other specific tasks. Home-based jobs are most often found in sales, recruiting, at companies with a heavy or fluctuating workload, companies with a need to cover phones around-the-clock, and companies that require medical or legal transcription.

In a home-based business you work independently and control most of your decisions, priorities, and time. You pay yourself based on the work that is completed and/or the products and services sold. The opportunities for running a home-based business continue to grow. Many people have run successful home-based secretarial, Web design, bookkeeping, childcare, training, coaching, counseling, freelance writing, or marketing businesses. Others have found success in the various multilevel marketing and direct marketing opportunities that are out there (e.g., Amway®, Tupperware®, Avon®, Big Planet®, Pampered Chef®, ReLiv®). You can also earn some extra cash by doing things such as secret shopping, taking surveys, surfing the Internet for cash and prizes, or registering for various affiliate programs on-line and getting paid for your referrals.

To succeed in any working-from-home arrangement, you must be self-motivated, dedicated, goal-oriented, persistent, and disciplined. You must also be willing to take risks. It takes a lot of organization and planning to work at home; there are numerous distractions when you work from home. You'll need to minimize and handle distractions like the phone, television, refrigerator, magazines, on-line games, laundry, pets, kids, and neighbors in order to accomplish your goals. If you are unable to focus at home, then a more traditional job may be better for you.

Working from home can supplement your family income or it can be the primary source to run the household. Most people with kids who choose to work from home do it because they are passionate about spending more time with their family and because the lifestyle appeals to them. Working from home comes with advantages such as independence, freedom, no commute, and no office politics. However, working from home isn't for everyone; those who have succeeded have evaluated the pros and cons for them, selected work they enjoy, and have established the workspace and time to accomplish their dreams.

Related Activity: Decide the best home-based work opportunities for you by getting in touch with your passions and identifying your skills. Seek to fulfill a need in the market so that you have more opportunities to succeed. Evaluate your family and whether the work you want to do will be a good fit for their situation. And, watch out for scams—they are abundant!

If you choose a home-based job, search in your local yellow pages and on-line directories for companies that may need your services. Look for on-line job banks that may need data entry services. Use the search engines on the Internet to find opportunities for "freelance" and "telecommuting" work. Network with business owners and get the word out on how you can help them.

If you decide to pursue a home-based business you can become a distributor or representative for a company or you can proposition a manufacturer or wholesaler to sell their products directly. You can create an on-line business as an affiliate program, selling products/services, or offering valuable resources for a fee. If you are good at Web design, you can create Web pages and/or offer your services to Webmasters. If you have a hobby or special talent, you may be able to turn it into a profitable business. If you have extremely good skills in an area, you can train or tutor others to help them develop their skills.

Keep in mind that working from home and taking care of your home and family simultaneously is like working two full-time jobs for half the pay!

Recommended Resources

1. *Best Home Businesses For The 21st Century: The Inside Information You Need To Know To Select A Home-Based Business That's Right For You*, by Paul and Sarah Edwards (J.P. Tarcher, 1999)
2. *Mompreneurs: A Mother's Practical Step-by-Step Guide To Work-At-Home Success* by Ellen H. Parlapiano and Patricia Cobe (Berkley Publishing Group, 1996)
3. *The Complete Idiot's Guide To Starting A Home-Based Business* by Barbara Welton (Alpha Books, 2000)
4. *The Stay-At-Home Mom's Guide To Making Money: How To Create The Business That's Right For You Using The Skills And Interests You Already Have* by Liz Folger (Prima Publishing, 2000)
5. *Home-Based Working Moms Inc.* (HBWM.com) is a professional association and on-line community of parents who work at home and those who would like to. There are many resources available at their site. Check out the "Work-at-Home Kit." It includes a workbook, home business book, membership and many other exciting and helpful items.

> *A baby is born with a need to be loved—and never outgrows it.*
> *~ Frank A. Clark*

TIP # 70 - PUT YOUR CAREER ON HOLD AS YOU RAISE YOUR FAMILY

Some parents take time off from their career to care full-time for their children. Although this isn't an option for some, there are plenty who wish they could find a way to make it happen. Those who have been committed to their career often have mixed feelings about the decision to leave their job. A sense of satisfaction and fulfillment is achieved from working.

It's important to listen to your heart when making this type of decision. When you are yearning to be at home with your kids, take the time to compute what it is costing you to be at work, financially and emotionally. When you subtract the cost of childcare from your take home pay, you may realize that there's not a big difference.

Some parents who have made these choices say that it was an adjustment at first; they felt like they were missing something. They were concerned about losing their skills and contacts in their chosen profession. They feared that there would be no work for them in the future if they choose to return to the working world. They also feared lack of respect from others who are employed outside the home.

When raising an infant, there is a lot of downtime. The baby normally naps a few hours during the day. This may be boring for you if you are used to a different lifestyle. You may feel lonely if many of your friends are busy working. You'll need to reach out and create some new friendships. There are support groups, organizations, playgroups, and other avenues to meet new people. You can also find things to do at home to help keep up your skills and earn money (e.g., home-based businesses, on-line classes). This may provide you with a new career to turn to as your children get older and start school.

In time, you will probably adjust to your new life and gain enjoyment from some of the more simple pleasures. The beginning of your child's life does not need to mean the end of your professional life. You can concentrate on raising your family, find opportunities to keep up with your career skills, build new skills, or whatever you like. If you think you might return to work someday, it's important to stay current in your field or learn a new one. To accomplish this, you can work part-time in your field, read professional journals, network with former colleagues, get involved with trade associations, seek out Web sites that focus on your occupation or industry, take classes, or attend seminars in-person or on-line.

Related Activity: Consider your reasons for working and your desires to stay at home with your children. Be sure to consider every aspect when deciding whether or not to stay home with your children. Get in touch with your feelings and your fears. If you yearn to be at home with your children, find a way to make it happen. If your expenses are far too high, drastically cut your budget and seek ways to simplify your life. If leaving the working world is clearly not an option, and you have a strong desire to be home with your children, explore work alternatives that will at least provide you with more time to be with your children (see Tips #65–70). Only you know what is best for you and your family, don't let anyone else decide. If staying home with your children is your goal, find a way to make it work.

Recommended Resources

1. *Keeping The Baby Alive Till Your Wife Gets Home: The Tough New 'How-To' For 21st Century Dads* by Walter Roark (Clearing Skies Press, 2002)
2. *Staying Home: From Full-Time Professional To Full-Time Parent* by Darcie Sanders and Martha M Bullen (Spencer & Waters, 1999)
3. *You Can Afford To Stay Home With Your Kids: A Step-By-Step Guide For Converting Your Family From Two Incomes To One* by Malia McCawley Wyckoff and Mary Snyder (Career Press, 1999)

Professional Skills

*Don't say you don't have enough time. You have exactly the same
number of hours per day that were given to Helen Keller, Pasteur,
Michelangelo, Mother Teresa, Leonardo da Vinci, Thomas Jefferson,
and Albert Einstein.*

~ *H. Jackson Brown*

TIP # 71 - RECLAIM WASTED TIME AT WORK

By working longer hours you may feel that you'll get more done, but
the key real is working *smarter*. The average person wastes
approximately five hours every week socializing, making personal
phone calls, searching for files, and surfing the Web. It's important to
utilize your time wisely and be productive at work. Just 15 minutes of
reclaimed time here and there can add up to big, noticeable
improvements and changes down the line.

If you can eliminate, or at least alleviate, some of your biggest time
wasters, and use the time to get more done during your "normal"
work hours, you'll more likely go home (without carrying a briefcase
full of work) when everyone else does.

Start by looking at the way you plan your day and approach your
work. Prioritize to get the most important tasks done early while your
energy level is still high. Eliminate those tasks that really are not
necessary and delegate those items that should really be done by
someone else. Multitask minor activities, when possible, such as
opening e-mail while returning phone calls. Break down larger
projects into smaller tasks.

Related Activity: Track how you use your time this week by keeping
a log of the time spent on various activities. Determine where you are
not using time efficiently. How are you spending that time? What
behaviors and actions can you change to make better use of your
time? Identify ways you can improve your performance and results.

Recommended Resources

1. *Eat That Frog!: 21 Great Ways to Stop Procrastinating And Get More Done In Less Time* by Brian Tracy (Audio Literature, 2001)
2. *The Complete Idiot's Guide to Managing Your Time* by Jeff Davidson (Alpha Books, 2002)
3. *The One Minute Manager* by Spencer Johnson with Kenneth H. Blanchard (Berkley Publishing Group, 1983)
4. *Simplify Your Work Life: Ways To Change The Way You Work So You Have More Time To Live* by Elaine St. James (Hyperion Press, 2001)

Work Efficiently and Productively!

> *I long to accomplish a great and noble task, but it is my chief duty to accomplish small tasks as if they were great and noble.*
>
> ~ *Helen Keller*

TIP # 72 - AVOID SUPERFLUOUS MULTITASKING

By continuously multitasking you are missing out on what might well be the most precious moments of your day.

A while back I had the pleasure of watching some apparently busy working families when I took my children to the park. Many of the moms I observed became so engrossed in conversations on their cell phones, work they had brought along with them, or books they were reading that they missed the simple pleasure of watching their child make a new friend or giggle uncontrollably while they explored the adventures in the park.

Technology is enabling multitasking to occur more so than it did many years ago when things were simpler. When we try to accomplish as much as is physically possible at any one time, we are doing too many things at once and our families and jobs (and we) may all suffer as a result. Just as an over-trained athlete's body stops performing at its peak level, our brains, when overburdened, do the same thing.

Certain mindless activities may be performed simultaneously; however, when you are performing two or more tasks that are distinct and difficult, your brain cannot properly reason, plan, or process the information. The brain functions in a way that leaves incomplete tasks open while working on another task.

Related Activity: Re-look at how you're organizing and performing your tasks. Enjoy the power of focusing on just one distinct activity and completing it free of distractions. Celebrate the higher quality of your efforts!

> *The secret of getting ahead is getting started. The secret of getting started is breaking your complex overwhelming tasks into small manageable tasks, and then starting on the first one.*
>
> *~ Mark Twain*

TIP # 73 - ELIMINATE UNNECESSARY TASKS

Begin working smarter rather than working harder! Start asking yourself whether you really need to do all that you are doing. Look at your daily, weekly, and monthly tasks to determine what you can eliminate. Often you delegate tasks and activities, but this time the challenge is even bigger—it's time to simply stop doing them.

It's so easy to get caught up in what you are doing that you never stop to determine if what you are doing is even worthwhile. If there's a report you've been generating regularly, is anyone reading it? What are they doing with it? What would happen if they didn't receive that report anymore?

A colleague of mine worked diligently every week to deliver a report each Friday morning. She often sacrificed time with her family on Thursday nights to ensure that the report was submitted on time. After thinking about how the report was and was not being used, she decided to play a game; she stopped doing the report. And, surprisingly, it took four months before anyone noticed! The person who noticed simply asked what ever happened to it, but he had no need for the data it contained.

Related Activity: Find a few things in your work or personal life that you can stop doing. Step back to determine whether or not you really need to be doing everything you are doing. Start by taking an inventory of the tasks you complete for work. Be brutally honest and detach from the tasks...question the value of each and determine which ones you can stop doing. Then, create a list of your household tasks and do the same thing. Be persistent! This will not be easy, but when you're done, you'll have more time and energy available for the *meaningful* tasks in your life.

Recommended Resources

1. *Getting Things Done: The Art Of Stress-Free Productivity* by David Allen (Viking Press, 2001)
2. *Simplify Your Work Life: Ways To Change The Way You Work So You Have More Time To Live* by Elaine St. James (Hyperion, 2002)
3. *Organized To Be Your Best! Simplify And Improve How You Work* by Susan Silver (Adams Hall Publishing, 2000)

Success for Super Busy Parents

Key Essential #7

SIMPLIFY YOUR LIFE

Stop overworking and overcommitting. Let go of unrealistic expectations of perfection and focus on progress instead. Gain more satisfaction in life by optimizing your time & resources to get more of what you want. Determine if you're really as busy as you think you are.

> *Patience, persistence and perspiration make an unbeatable combination for success.*
>
> *~ Napolean Hill*

TIP # 74 - MANAGE STRESS AT WORK

The stress you feel comes from the importance, significance, or emphasis you place on something; things and people that matter most to you generate higher levels of stress. Stress is a mentally or emotionally disruptive influence. It can come from external sources based on your involvement in the world and with other people, or it can come from internal sources based on your beliefs, attitudes, and behavior.

Everybody responds to stress in his own way. The effects of stress generally fall into three categories:

- Physical signs and symptoms
- Thoughts and feelings
- Behaviors

Although you need a certain amount of stress in your life to keep it stimulating, challenging, and exciting, too much stress can seriously affect your physical and mental well-being. Work stresses tend to come from too much work, incorrect fits, lack of job security, wrong skills or knowledge, poor communication, interpersonal conflicts, or other people-related issues.

You can more effectively manage work-related stresses if you:

Quit worrying	Handle anger	Define your limits
Stop hurrying	Lower noise levels	Do physical exercise
Align your life	Keep skills current	Eliminate adrenaline
Be positive	Resolve conflicts	Get feedback
Smile/Laugh	Forget envy	Practice self-care
Manage your time	Use mental imagery & breathing to relax	Talk to a confidant

You probably know in advance what types of situations are likely to be stressful for you. Prepare for worst-case scenarios by identifying situations that cause you the most stress. By increasing your confidence and ability to handle situations, you will be more prepared to manage the accompanying stress. Recognize several ways you can cope with anticipated stresses. Be aware of your symptoms of stress and monitor your behavior and reactions.

Related Activity: Describe at least one source of stress that most commonly interferes with your work-related tasks. Explore ways to more effectively cope with this issue—what strategies can you use to more effectively cope? What stress management techniques from work can you bring home? Which can you bring from home to work?

Recommended Resources

1. *Don't Sweat The Small Stuff At Work: Simple Ways To Minimize Stress And Conflict While Bringing Out The Best In Yourself And Others* by Richard Carlson (Hyperion Press, 1998)
2. *Stress Management For Dummies* by Alan Elkin (John Wiley & Sons, 1999)
3. *Stress Reduction & Creative Meditations for Work & Career* by Marc Allen and Jon Bernoff (*audiotape by* New World Library, 1999)
4. *Who Moved My Cheese? An Amazing Way To Deal With Change In Your Work And In Your Life* by Spencer Johnson (Putnam Publishing Group, 1998)

Integrity is telling myself the truth. And honesty is telling the truth to other people.

~ *Spencer Johnson*

TIP # 75 - ACT WITH INTEGRITY

Integrity involves the inherent knowledge of what's right and wrong, the ability to avoid the wrong, and the willingness to stand up for what is right. Being authentic at work and following through on your commitments is a demonstration of your integrity.

From an organizational perspective, integrity often starts with the establishment of trust between you and your co-workers. When you model ethical behavior, you build trust by being consistent, communicating clearly and honestly, making and keeping promises, admitting your mistakes, setting good examples, recognizing internal conflicts, standing up for what you believe in, protecting confidences, and treating others with respect. Operating with integrity is a *choice* that reflects what is right or healthy for you; we each have our own degree of integrity within our life.

You can be either in integrity or out of integrity. You would probably be out of integrity at work if you:

- work excessive hours while saying family is your priority.
- don't apologize when you have wronged someone.
- steal someone else's idea without giving them credit.
- work at the wrong job (or career).
- over-promise results.
- put yourself at undue physical risk.
- live in fear.
- misrepresent yourself.
- lie to get what you want.

When you are out of integrity things don't feel right, you don't feel whole, and you usually lack a level of harmony in your life.

Integrity is the result of your actions being in alignment with your beliefs and when you take full responsibility for yourself.

Related Activity: Examine where you are feeling out of integrity. List the items, actions, habits, or activities that keep you out of integrity. How do you know when you are out of integrity? Identify changes you can make to restore your integrity in each case. Then identify actions or solutions you can take to bring you back to integrity. Start restoring your integrity so that you can experience more richness and wholeness in your life. When you begin restoring your integrity you will achieve the results you want in your life with more energy and less effort.

Recommended Resource

1. *A Rock And A Hard Place: How To Make Ethical Business Decisions When The Choices Are Tough* by Kent Hodgson (Amacon, 1992)
2. *Focal Point: A Proven System To Simplify Your Life, Double Your Productivity, And Achieve All Your Goals* by Brian Tracy (Amacon, 2001)
3. *The 100 Absolutely Unbreakable Laws Of Business Success* by Brian Tracy (Berrett-Koehler Publishing, 2000)
4. *The Balanced Scorecard: Translating Strategy Into Action* by Robert S. Kaplan and David P. Norton (Harvard Business School Publishing, 1996)
5. *Winning With Integrity: Getting What You Want Without Selling Your Soul* by Leigh Steinberg and Michael D'Orso (Times Books, 1999)

Concluding Thoughts...

As I finish writing this book, I've already begun the next book in the series and am contemplating a companion workbook that takes you through the related activities that help you create more balance in your life, love, family, and work.

I found great joy writing this book and getting feedback from those who've read my weekly e-newsletter and draft copies of my manuscript. I encourage your suggestions and criticisms, and welcome them through e-mail at natalie@superbusyparent.com. I had to let go of perfection in my life and in the pages of this book in order to complete this phenomenal project. Please let me know if you see anything that can be improved or corrected.

In the future, I'd like to host conversations and more sharing of ideas and inspiration between *super busy* working parents. You have an infinite amount of wisdom and capability of growing your own greatness. I'd like to help you get to your optimum levels so you can experience more fulfillment and joy.

You may arrange to have me visit your workplace or social organization as a guest to speak about topics related to this book. I am available for workshops, training sessions, group coaching and one-on-one coaching, as well as professional consultation.

To order additional copies of this book as gifts, or to bulk order, please visit the book store at www.infinitypublishing.com. This book makes an excellent gift for employers to give to all their working parents. (You can even customize the book with a letter from your CEO when ordering bulk quantities!)

NOTES

NOTES

NOTES

NOTES

NOTES

Appendix 1

MY FAVORITE TOP 10 LISTS

TOP 10 TIPS
FOR
BALANCING WORK/FAMILY LIFE

There is no single formula for attaining a balanced life. How you combine your career, spouse/significant other, children, friends, and self into an integrated whole is a personal process because it's actually a combination of decisions. The key is to develop creative solutions as you approach the challenges of balancing the responsibilities and joys of your multiple roles. Some of the same skills and strategies you use at work such as planning, organizing, communicating, setting limits, and delegating can be used effectively on the home-front for achieving a satisfying, fulfilling well-balanced life both personally and professionally.

1. BUILD A SUPPORT NETWORK (see Tip # 46)
Ask for help and allow yourself to be helped and contributed to. Get your children involved—work together as a team. Recruit friends, family, neighbors, bosses, or your work colleagues and ask for their support. Create back-up and emergency plans; always have a contingency.

2. LET GO OF GUILT (see Tip # 22)
Guilt is one of the greatest wastes of emotional energy. It causes you to become immobilized because you are dwelling on the past. Guilt can be very debilitating. By introducing logic to help counter-balance guilt, you can stay on course.

3. ESTABLISH LIMITS AND BOUNDARIES (see Tip #19)
Boundaries are an imaginary line of protection that you draw around yourself. They are about protecting you from other people's actions. Boundaries and limits help you take charge of your time and space and get in touch with your feelings. They express the extent of your responsibilities and power and show others what you are willing to do or accept. Determine for yourself what is acceptable and unacceptable behavior from other people. Without limits it's difficult to say "no" (see Tip #21).

185

4. DETERMINE YOUR OWN STANDARDS

Get rid of the notion of being a perfectionist. Wean yourself by making compromises; figure out where the best places to make the compromises are without short-changing yourself, your spouse, your children, or your boss. Live by your own standards rather than someone else's. Standards are about YOU and refer to the behavior and actions you are willing to hold yourself to.

5. CREATE TIME FOR YOURSELF (see Tip #10)

Being a good parent, partner, and professional means being good to yourself first. Use your mind to make some affirmations for yourself. Find ways to relax, relieve tension, and minimize stress. Taking some time off for yourself will not only benefit you, but it will benefit your family tremendously!

6. GET ORGANIZED (see Tip #14)

Set priorities, work smarter not harder, delegate (and really let go!). Create lists and save them for reuse. Keep a main calendar centrally located to post everyone's activities.

7. BE FLEXIBLE

Forgive yourself when things don't get done. Understand that with children things change at a moment's notice. Be ready and willing to assume responsibility for any of the tasks that need to get done at any time. Never get too comfortable, because as soon as you seem to get things under control, they change! Also, realize that in order to achieve success, many people have had to give up their original goals and substitute new ones with different but equal challenges. Negotiate for what you need.

8. ENJOY HIGH-QUALITY FAMILY TIME (see Tips #36-40)

Spend quality/focused time with your family. Give them your full attention. Develop rituals you can all look forward to. Create relationships with your spouse and children that are not incidental, but instrumental to your success.

9. **FIND RELIABLE CHILDCARE** (see Tip #29)
Leave your kids in capable hands. Find someone you feel comfortable with. If you're feeling ambivalent about working or about leaving your child do not show it—your child (at any age) will pick up on it. Feel proud when you've found someone who fits into your needs. Get involved with your child's care providers by communicating frequently and observing interactions between caregiver and your child.

10. **ACHIEVE AN INTEGRATED LIFE** (see Tip #50)
Keep things in perspective. Create harmony in your life—a mixture of work, family, and friends. Remember, there is no single formula for balance. How you combine your spouse, children, and career is a personal process.

TOP 10 WAYS TO NOURISH YOURSELF

Revive and re-nourish yourself by carving out some time in your busy schedule because you not only deserve it, but you need it in order to truly be productive in all aspects of your life. The absence of time for you is both a physical and emotional health hazard!

1. HALF-HOUR—FULL HOUR MASSAGE
Any type of bodywork is an important measure for restoring balance, getting circulation flowing, decreasing tension, and increasing your energy level. If you find you cannot afford one, look for massage schools, which offer significant discounts.

2. FACIAL OR MAKEOVER
Let the real you shine through and be reflected when you glimpse in the mirror. Does your image reflect who you are?

3. PRIVATE LESSONS
Learn something new or improve something you'd like to do better by hiring a private tutor.

4. FULFILL A LONG-TERM FANTASY/DREAM
Do something you've always dreamed of doing but never dared to try. See what it feels like to step through the fear and whatever else has been holding you back.

5. DO SOMETHING SPIRITUAL
Spirituality connotes differing meanings for each person. Find a way that you can personally connect to the universe. Listen to your "inner voice" or "wise self" as it guides you with the answers. Look mystically into your future using palm reading or tarot cards, if you dare!

6. GET YOUR COLORS ANALYZED
Certain colors are more flattering on you than others. Why not find out which colors work best for you and then update your wardrobe (and makeup) to reflect your best. You'll undoubtedly feel more confident when you look great.

7. HIRE HELP TO DO WHAT YOU DON'T WANT TO
There are so many tasks that need to get done that would better be served by having someone else do them. Whether it be grocery shopping, cleaning, standing in endless lines for registrations/license renewals, cooking, driving, running errands, etc. there is most · probably a professional service out there that's willing to do it for you for a fee. Be creative and try it out!

8. PICK UP A COMPLETE DINNER
Get your dinner from the gourmet shop or hire a personal chef to prepare a meal at home. Why not dine on scrumptious food without the bother of shopping, preparing and cleaning up. Enjoy the meal with a special someone(s) and double the value.

9. PLAY HOOKY FROM WORK
Take the day off from work to do whatever you want to do either alone or with someone special while taking advantage of the smaller weekday crowds.

10. HIBERNATE AT HOME
Why not enjoy the quiet while everyone else is out and relax and do whatever comes to mind or nothing at all...guilt-free.

TOP 10 GUILT BUSTERS

Guilt is a great waste of emotional energy. It causes us to become immobilized in the present because we are dwelling on the past. Guilt can be very debilitating. It often brings productive thoughts and actions to a standstill. Introducing logic helps counter-balance guilt and helps us stay on course.

A key point about guilt is that it is a condition and not a feeling. Using guilt as a feeling masks deeper emotions and the identity of a problem.

1. LIVE IN THE HERE AND NOW
Make the present *perfect*. Do not expend your energy dwelling on what you should've, could've, might've done in the past. The present is a gift, enjoy it!

2. SAY "NO" MORE OFTEN (see Tip #21)
Establish a list of what's absolutely important to you. Do very few things you resent or strongly prefer not to do. Refer to this list as a reminder of your priorities.

3. REALIZE YOU CAN'T DO IT ALL
Delegate more often. Stop trying to be everything to everybody. Avoid the perfectionism attitude.

4. PUT THINGS IN PERSPECTIVE
Determine whose standards you're trying to live up to.

5. BE SECURE WITH WHAT'S IMPORTANT TO YOU AND YOUR CHOICES
Taking action is almost always a better choice than doing nothing. Be aligned with "who" you are and base your decisions on that.

6. TAKE GOOD CARE OF YOURSELF
Do at least one thing each day just because you want to or feel like it. If necessary, write yourself a permission slip that permits you to do something special just for you.

7. IDENTIFY THE REAL PROBLEM
Take a close look at why you feel guilty and work toward resolving the problem versus a symptom.

8. LEARN TO LET GO
Stop beating yourself up about something that's happened in the past. Once it's over let it be over and don't keep re-living it and stressing or worrying about how it could've been different.

9. SET YOURSELF UP FOR SUCCESS
Rather than establishing many far-reaching goals, set small attainable goals that lead to a larger "stretch" goal. Celebrate your accomplishments along the way. Try, also, to take just one project at a time to avoid feeling overwhelmed and guilty because you messed up on something.

10. LIGHTEN UP! HAVE FUN
Stop taking yourself (and others) so seriously. Learn to laugh at yourself more freely. Smile more often. Find joy in simple activities.

TOP 10 TIPS
FOR
UTILIZING TIME MORE EFFICIENTLY

Time is a priceless treasure. Treasure every moment you have and remember that time waits for no one. You cannot make six minutes out of five just because you managed your time effectively. Each day you are given the gift of a new day, 24 hours. Utilize it the best way possible and don't let it slip through your fingers. You cannot ever replace lost time. You can't buy time or save time; you can only spend time...once it's spent it's gone!

1. PRIORITIZE
Determine what's truly important to you. Schedule those items and activities first and then schedule everything else around it to the extent you can (noting some things are scheduled at precise times and there is less flexibility). Don't' cancel the important (not urgent) activities for any reason.

2. PLAN
Planning is a crucial skill when you want to accomplish something. However, it's often the first thing forgotten when things get hectic and busy. Planning magnifies time by providing direction and enhancing productivity. Life is simpler and easier when planned out.

3. DELEGATE
Anything you're doing that could be handled by someone else could be delegated. If you look at your time in terms of dollars you can compute how much your time is actually worth. Then, you may be more willing to delegate the more routine tasks or chores, and free your time and energy for your top priorities and high-level work.

4. REPLICATE YOURSELF
No, you cannot actually duplicate yourself or add more arms and legs but the fact is, you can find someone who is just as good as you in a given task. You can also automate or systematize some of your routine tasks. Replication is about increasing your results without expending more time and energy.

5. SET GOALS
(HAVE STRONG INTENTIONS/A VISION/DIRECTION)
Establish specific goals on a daily basis to help you decide what you want to achieve with your time and to set targets that will lead you to achieving them more regularly. Setting goals may be very effective at raising your self-confidence by focusing on progress. In addition to having increased performance levels, goals will keep you more highly motivated.

6. STRUCTURE YOUR DAY
As individuals, we all have peak performance times. Learn when it's your best time for greatest productivity, quiet thinking, or exercise and arrange your day accordingly to maximize your personal advantage. Each person has an "ideal" work style that operates as a function of who they are, their body, and personality type. Begin to understand and honor that style in you and you'll be more effective as a result.

7. VALUE YOUR TIME
If you demonstrate by your words, actions, and commitments that your time is important to you, others will recognize how you value your time and will show more respect of it. On the other hand, if you don't value your time, don't expect anyone else to. By valuing your time, you are in essence valuing your self. One important thing to remember is that the only way others will respect your time is if YOU respect your time.

8. GET ORGANIZED
Have a place for everything both in your office and in your home; it pays off in less wasted time searching for something you just can't seem to find. Over the years, studies have shown that people working with a messy desk or work area spend an average 1.5 hours per day looking for or being distracted by things (at just minutes at a time!) In addition, create a (centralized) list of what you want to get done. Manage the activities and projects you can control; clearly distinguish between what is and is not actionable. You can also group activities that can be done simultaneously or on the same trip out. The key is to focus on about six activities you wish to accomplish at the start of each day and to keep your list manageable.

9. BECOME FULLY FOCUSED IN THE MOMENT
By focusing on what you are doing you permit yourself to get absorbed in the activity, be more relaxed and increase your creativity. Fact is, when you allow yourself to become totally focused on what you are doing at the moment, a freer flowing momentum occurs and you actually get the job done faster and easier. Be deliberate in how you use your time. Make the present perfect rather than splitting your attention.

10. ELIMINATE TIME WASTERS
Yes, we all have them in our life—interruptions, distractions, poor planning, ineffective behaviors and attitudes, and over-commitments. Rather than letting time control you, take control of your time and your life by incorporating some of the tips listed above. Take personal responsibility for creating stronger boundaries and communicating them to your colleagues, bosses, significant others, and family.

TOP 10 WAYS
TO
FIT FITNESS INTO YOUR "TOO" BUSY SCHEDULE

If you think you don't have time for fitness because your children need your attention, or work seems to be consuming all your time, or you have absolutely no energy left by the end of the day to even think about exercising, perhaps it's time you look at the priorities in your life. Ask yourself... do you want to feel good and have more energy? Have easier weight control? Have an improved appearance? Less stress? Better health? Increased sense of well being? Enhanced relaxation? If you answered yes to any of these questions, take a look at the tips below to see what strategies you can adapt in your daily life.

Exercise should be an enjoyable part of your everyday life. If it is not, you will not continue with it. Choose activities that you enjoy and that are readily accessible. Begin with a little increase of activity as a first step and then, over time you'll see that it becomes easier to do even more. A trim and healthy lifestyle can be enjoyed by adding incidental exercise to a busy schedule. Even your busiest schedule can have time for fitness activities. See how creative you can be with your schedule and your family.

(Note: Always consult your healthcare provider before beginning or changing your exercise routine. Work with a certified exercise instructor to learn how to exercise safely.)

1. STRETCH EVERY A.M.
Do wake-up stretches every morning for a few minutes. This energizes your muscles and limbers your joints.

2. STEP IT UP
Take the stairs instead of the elevator or escalator. If you live or work in a high-rise building, perhaps you could opt for getting off the elevator a few floors prior to your floor and walking the stairs the rest of the way.

3. WALK WITH A BUDDY
Take a 20–30 minute walk with a co-worker during your lunch hour. Having a buddy will help motivate you daily.

4. DO P.M. STRETCHING AND BREATHING EXERCISE
Take a stretch break in the afternoon to ward off fatigue and soreness from sitting too long. Practice deep-cleansing breathing exercises for about five minutes each afternoon.

5. PARK AND WALK
Rather than taking the first space in the parking lot, park further away and walk the distance. (NOTE: Make sure your parking lot is safe!)

6. EXERCISE YOUR CHORES AWAY
Do yard walk, rake the leaves, mop, dust, vacuum, walk the dog, etc. while enjoying the physical activity. Pop on some tunes if it helps brighten your mood to accompany these tasks.

7. HAVE THE FAMILY JOIN IN
Add no-cost, fun exercise activities to Sunday family outings. Rotate the selection and planning of the activities with each family member. Some examples include walking the beach, going for a bike ride, hiking up a mountain.

8. GO AEROBIC
Experiment with mini-aerobic workouts for 20–30 minutes at least three times a week. Some examples include following an exercise video, stair-climbing, cross-country skiing, walking, jogging, bike riding, dancing, and rowing. These activities strengthen your cardiovascular system and burn fat.

9. STRENGTH TRAINING
Strength training is important for your muscles and bones. Do 10–15 minutes 2–3 times a week. Follow a muscle conditioning video or join a gym.

10. SNACK SMARTLY
Don't wait till you're starving to eat. For a snack, try fresh fruit, yogurt, raw vegetables, juice, or herb tea. Drink plenty of water throughout the day.

Top 10 Tips
For
Avoiding the Morning Mayhem

Mornings are chaotic in many households but when you add your work, spouse, children, school, and daycare to the mixture havoc can take over a normally peaceful environment. Unfortunately, this hurried frantic pace sets the tone for the rest of the day. When your morning activities run smoothly and you're out the door with ample time, it can make a significant difference the whole rest of the day. As so many of us know first-hand, how the morning starts can make or break a day for children and parents with things to do and places to be.

Here are a few tips I've incorporated into my own life and picked up from parents and experts along the way:

1. Prepare the Night Before
Do as much as you can before heading off to sleep so that your mornings feel less rushed. For example, lay out your clothes (and that of your young children); pack school schoolbags, briefcases, diaper bags, etc; put all essential items right by the exit door; prepare lunches; and, set out breakfast dishes. Plan your next day the night before, too. No matter how tired you are, you'll sleep better if you know you have tomorrow already organized. The key is to eliminate as many chores and decisions from your morning as possible.

2. Awaken Earlier
Set the alarm clock about a half hour earlier and enjoy the less hurried pace. Remember, this pace sets the tone for the rest of the day. Get up ahead of the "crowd" and enjoy the quiet unhurried pace of the beginning of your day and may even give you the opportunity to carve out some private time for yourself.

3. Put on Your Watch First
Keep an eye on the time by having it handy upon your wrist. This will help you monitor and keep better track of your time.

4. KEEP YOUR HOUSEHOLD ORGANIZED
Have a place you always put your keys, gloves, shoes, coat, briefcase, important papers, and other essentials. That way you will not be spending time frantically searching for items on your way out the door. Some experts suggest using plastic tubs or decorated boxes labeled with each family member's name and leaving them by the door as the drop-off location.

5. PLAY A GAME
Have a race to see who can get dressed first, finish eating, brush teeth, put on shoes, and get in the car. Make it fun and noncompetitive. Give everyone a chance to be the "winner" and offer praise for getting done so quickly. Your praise and positive reinforcement will encourage your children to continue meeting their goals more than criticism and harsh judgment.

6. HAVE AN ASSORTMENT OF CONVENIENT HEALTHY FOODS ON HAND FOR BREAKFAST
Rather than skipping breakfast because you're running behind and don't have adequate time, take the time to fuel up on instant oatmeal, dry cereals, cereal bars, toaster cakes, bagels, fruits, trail mix, frozen waffles, or other quick fixes. Breakfast can be fast and nutritious if you plan ahead and remain fully stocked with your family's favorites.

7. SIMPLIFY CLOTHING
Avoid fabrics that are hard to care for. Stick to color schemes and mix/match outfits. Group similar items together in the closet to make them easy to match up. Sew on buttons, fix zippers, and repair hems before hanging clothes back in your closet so that they are ready to be worn the next time you pull them out.

8. LET GO OF PERFECTION
Unless your house is listed on the market to be sold, it really doesn't have to be spotless before you leave the house everyday. From time to time allow yourself to leave with the beds unmade, dishes soaking in the sink or a few toys left out. It's not about lowering your standards but accepting your limitations.

9. ENLIST EVERYONE'S COOPERATION

Rather than attempting to do it all, get everyone involved in the goal of having a less hectic morning. Request suggestions and share responsibilities. Empower the "home" team to achieve the goal blissfully each day. Show your kids how to do more things for themselves. Encourage greater independence in your children; make mornings a balance between intervention and independence. Keep distractions such as the TV and favorite toys out of sight or at least kept to a minimum. Praise the successes and accomplishments along the way because your words of praise will encourage your children to continue to meet their goals.

10. GET ADEQUATE SLEEP

Sticking to a bedtime routine can give your child a sense of comfort. However, no matter how well-prepared you and your children are for the morning, if your child doesn't get enough sleep the night before, you'll definitely be off to a rough start of the day. Make sure everyone goes to sleep early enough the night before to get adequate rest. After a good night's sleep you'll all be ready to take on more of the daily grind. Make sure your beds are comfortable and you've established an environment to support a good night's sleep. Keep to your schedule as much as possible, even on weekends and vacations.

TOP 10 TIPS
FOR
WORKING FROM A HOME-BASED OFFICE

There is a significant rise in the number of people performing home-based work. Below are some simple tips that may help you become more productive and effective.

1. DELINEATE OFFICE SPACE
Create the space you will call your office and make it off limits to others, if at all possible. Make sure this space is comfortable and inspiring to you. Avoid clutter because it detracts from your energy and motivation levels.

2. ESTABLISH AND COMMUNICATE WORK HOURS
Avoid distractions and interruptions by letting people know when you are working. Create boundaries and standards and make sure you honor them (expect others to honor them, as well). Don't deal with personal problems during work hours. Instead, set aside specific times for taking care of personal issues.

3. CREATE AN ABUNDANCE OF SUPPLIES
Make sure you have enough paper, staples, paperclips, tape, toner, postage stamps, and other essential supplies on hand so you don't run out in the middle of something big. The last thing you need during a busy time is to have to stop everything to run out to pick up something. Plan ahead!

4. HAVE AND MAINTAIN THE NECESSARY EQUIPMENT
Determine what you'll need in your office to function at optimal level. Purchase, rent, lease, or borrow whatever you need and be sure to keep it in tip-top shape.

5. BACK UP YOUR FILES PERIODICALLY
Avoid a natural disaster. Computers do crash. Make sure that when yours does you have all the pertinent data you need to get yourself back into business fast.

6. **BUILD A NETWORK OF RESOURCES TO TURN TO FOR HELP**
You can't possibly do everything yourself! Seek support from your family and friends. Also, develop a team of professionals you can turn to or refer others to for their expertise. Find some experts and models to guide and inspire you, as well.

7. **UTILIZE NETWORKING OPPORTUNITIES**
Avoid feeling isolated. Join a personal or professional networking group, create a mastermind group, meet a colleague for lunch, partner with someone, volunteer, join a local gym, attend classes or seminars, connect with former co-workers, make contacts on-line through the Internet, give talks to professional organizations, or conduct a workshop.

8. **SET CLEARLY DEFINED, ACHIEVABLE BUSINESS GOALS**
Write down your goals and keep them visible. Be sure they are exact, attainable, realistic, and trackable. Rather than establishing many far-reaching goals, set small reachable goals that lead to larger, more distant goals. Stay in action. Celebrate your accomplishments along the way.

9. **ALLOW YOURSELF TO ENJOY YOUR "COMMUTE"**
Use the additional time you have gained by not having to drive to the office to enhance your personal life. Take a break and do something you enjoy. Be a good boss and take care of yourself physically and emotionally.

10. **ESTABLISH SYSTEMS FOR MANAGING CHILDCARE AND HOUSEHOLD CHORES**
Get reliable childcare whether it's in your home or outside. It's important to keep the children away from you when you are working so that you have the opportunity to have focused, creative, and productive work time free of distractions and interruptions. Create back-up arrangements, as well. Get a low cost housecleaner to assist with the household chores or use other effective means to keep your house in order (e.g., delegate some responsibilities, divide household chores, let go of perfection!).

Appendix 2

ADDITIONAL RESOURCES

Additional Resources

This section contains a list of some of my favorite Web sites that were available at the time of publication. This list is not inclusive and some of the sites may have moved or are no longer be available. If you have a site to recommend (or remove), please contact the author at natalie@superbusyparent.com.

Web sites for Parenting:
- www.ala.org/parentspage/greatsites
- www.epregnancy.com
- www.everythingforparents.com
- www.familyandhome.org
- www.familyfun.com
- www.frugalliving.com
- www.frugalmoms.com
- www.localmom.com
- www.myfamily.com
- www.parentinghumor.com
- www.parentingstages.com
- www.parentingteens.com
- www.parentsoup.com
- www.parents-talk.com
- www.thebabycorner.com
- www.tnpc.com

Web sites for Dads:
- www.dadstoday.com
- www.dadmag.com
- www.dadstayshome.com
- www.dualcareerdads.com
- www.fatherhoodproject.org
- www.fathermag.com
- www.fathers.com
- www.fathersdirect.com
- www.newdads.com
- www.parentpreneurclub.com
- www.slowlane.com
- www.wahd.com

Web sites for Working Moms/Women:
- www.bluesuitmom.com
- www.briefcasemom.com
- www.clubmom.com
- www.freebiesforwomen.com
- www.generationmom.com
- www.hbwm.com
- www.info@wellness4u.com
- www.ivillage.com
- www.momsnetwork.com
- www.momson-line.com
- www.momsrefuge.com
- www.MoNews@oxygen.com
- www.myria.com
- www.NetWorkingMoms.com
- www.oxygen.com
- www.selfgrowth.com
- www.sheknows.com
- www.TheCyberMom.com
- www.transformingwork.com
- www.women.com
- www.WomenConnect.com
- www.womensforum.com
- www.womensleadership.com
- www.WorkingMother.com

Web sites for Children:
- www.disney.com
- www.afterschool.gov/kidsnteens.html
- www.beritsbest.comw
- www.geocities.com
- www.kids.discovery.com
- www.kidscom.com
- www.nasa.gov/kids.html
- www.nick.com
- www.nick.com
- www.pbs.org
- www.sikids.com

Web sites for Work Alternatives:
- iaia.essortment.com/jobsharingprin_oop.htm
- www.clubmom.com (look under "Tools" for their Work & Career checklists)
- www.flexible-recruitment.co.uk/on-line_jobshare_register.html (United Kingdom)
- www.jobshare.ie (Ireland)
- www.JobSharing.com
- www.momsworkathomesite.com
- www.sharegoals.com/home.asp
- www.womans-work.com/
- www.workathomecommunity.com/
- www.workoptions.com/jobshare.htm

About the Author

Natalie R. Gahrmann is a writer, success coach, speaker, trainer, business owner, and parent. She is featured on-line as the work/life expert at www.BlueSuitMom.com and the resident coach at www.NetWorkingMoms.com. In addition to being a graduate of Coach University, she has earned MA, BS, and AAS degrees. Natalie is a member of the International Coach Federation, Coachville, New Jersey Professional Coaches Association, Alliance of Work/Life Professionals, and the Central Jersey Women's Network. She is the leader of the Mom/Coach Special Interest Group, a community of coaches who are moms (and a few dads, too!), to help them integrate their multiple roles and responsibilities.

Natalie has appeared in local and national newspapers, parenting publications, Smart Money, Good Housekeeping, Redbook, and USA Today Careers Network. Her articles have been published on-line at MLM Woman Newsletter, Better Business Focus, Spencer Stuart, and Tumbler Ridge Assessment and Resource Service, among others. Natalie also produces a weekly e-newsletter for working parents which offers practical and timely tips to help master the challenges of work and life. (Send a blank email to superbusyparent-subscribe@yahoogroups.com to get your free subscription.)

A dedicated mother of two, Natalie chose to leave the corporate world after ten years to devote more time to raising her children while she runs her own private coaching and training company. As a Personal & Professional Success Coach, Natalie specializes in helping working parents create more fulfillment and joy in every facet of their life. She works with professionals, managers, and business owners one-on-one and in small groups to help them achieve their goals and dreams. She speaks to a wide variety of audiences on many of the topics you'll read about in this book. Her programs motivate participants to move from contemplating opportunities to making commitments and taking actions.

Natalie lives in New Jersey with her husband and two children and can be reached at her e-mail address: natalie@superbusyparent.com.

Succeeding as a Super Busy Parent makes an excellent gift!
To order additional copies for yourself or someone special.

FAX   Fax orders: (610) 941-9999

Phone Orders: Call toll free (877) BUY BOOK
                       Local Phone (610) 941-9999

Postal Orders: Copy and mail this form to:
                    Infinity Publishing
                    1094 New DeHaven Street, Suite 100
                    West Conshohocken, PA 19428-2713

Email: Info@buybooksontheweb.com
WEB: www.buybooksontheweb.com

*For orders outside of the US and Canada, please visit www.amazon.com

NAME_____

ADDRESS _____

CITY_____ STATE_____ ZIP_____

PHONE_____ FAX_____

E-MAIL_____

Payment: ☐ Check   ☐ Money Order ☐   Credit Card:

Card Number:_____

Name on Card:_____ Exp. Date:_____

Shipping & Handling: Include $4.50 for the first book, $1.00 for each
additional book (**free shipping on orders of 20 or more!!**)

Sales Tax: Please add **6%** for books shipped to Pennsylvania addresses

Quantity discounts are available!

To ***customize*** books for your organization or company, contact
Infinity publishing at (610) 941-9999

Succeeding as a Super Busy Parent makes an excellent gift!
To order additional copies for yourself or someone special.

FAX   **Fax orders**: (610) 941-9999

Phone Orders: Call toll free (877) BUY BOOK
Local Phone (610) 941-9999

Postal Orders: Copy and mail this form to:
Infinity Publishing
1094 New DeHaven Street, Suite 100
West Conshohocken, PA 19428-2713

Email: Info@buybooksontheweb.com
WEB: www.buybooksontheweb.com

*For orders outside of the US and Canada, please visit www.amazon.com

NAME_____

ADDRESS _____

CITY_____ STATE_____ ZIP_____

PHONE_____ FAX_____

E-MAIL_____

Payment: ☐ Check ☐ Money Order ☐ Credit Card:

Card Number:_____

Name on Card:_____ Exp. Date:_____

<u>Shipping & Handling:</u> Include $4.50 for the first book, $1.00 for each additional book (**free shipping on orders of 20 or more!!**)

<u>Sales Tax</u>: Please add **6%** for books shipped to Pennsylvania addresses

Quantity discounts are available!

To ***customize*** books for your organization or company, contact
Infinity publishing at (610) 941-9999